Seleni Python A Beginner's Guide

by

Pallavi Sharma

bpb

FIRST EDITION 2019
Copyright © BPB Publications, India
ISBN: 978-93-89328-813

Distributors:

BPB PUBLICATIONS
20, Ansari Road, Darya Ganj
New Delhi-110002
Ph: 23254990/23254991

DECCAN AGENCIES
4-3-329, Bank Street,
Hyderabad-500195
Ph: 24756967/24756400

MICRO MEDIA
Shop No. 5, Mahendra Chambers,
150 DN Rd. Next to Capital Cinema,
V.T. (C.S.T.) Station, MUMBAI-400 001
Ph: 22078296/22078297

BPB BOOK CENTRE
376 Old Lajpat Rai Market,
Delhi-110006
Ph: 23861747

Published by Manish Jain for BPB Publications, 20 Ansari Road, Darya Ganj, New Delhi-110002 and Printed by him at Repro India Ltd, Mumbai

Dedicated to

My Parents
Dr. Neelaksh Sharma & Dr. Manju Sharma
and
My Kids
Neeal & Maisha

About the Author

Pallavi has an overall professional experience of 14 years. She has worked in varied roles as a product/project manager in the presales team and marketing team for solutions on test automation tools. She holds two provisional patents along with other contributors for her work on building tool agnostic test automation framework solutions.

Currently, she is acting as a test automation coach, writer, speaker and owner at 5 Elements Learning where she collaborates and works with test automation enthusiasts across the globe. As an avid learner, she likes to keep herself updated to the latest trends and technologies.

She is a firm believer in larger good and likes to live by example. She volunteers her time for the organization eVidyaloka where she acts as a centre administrator. She is a lifetime member for the Jabarkhet forest reserve and People for Animals.

Reviewer

Afsana Atar is an expert software test professional, an Agile evangelist. She has over a decade's experience in the IT industry working with companies like Google, IBM, Principal Financial Group and Children's Hospital of Philadelphia. She is currently working with a financial trading and brokerage firm, Susquehanna International Group. She has managed several projects and ensured the delivery of critical projects which enabled customer success. She is also an international author with several books and publications on testing, test management and the tech industry in general. She extends her thought leadership to teams in a variety of domains from digital advertising, education & healthcare to the financial sector in banking, insurance & trading. She is a Certified Scrum Master (CSM), an Agile scrum practitioner and part of the scrum alliance community. She is also an international speaker and has been invited to an international conference in Brazil and the USA after great success of her book "Hands-On Test Management with JIRA".

Acknowledgement

First and foremost, I would like to thank Mr Manish Jain from BPB Publications for giving me this opportunity to write the book. I would also like to thank Nrip, Priyanka and all the people associated with this book. The entire team was very helpful and forthcoming in solving queries and making a first-time writer feel comfortable.

I would like to thank Mr. Pankaj Goel, CEO at CresTech, to introduce me to the world of Software Test Automation, to hold my hand and help me walk the path. I would also like to thank Dr. Naren Ramakrishnan, Director at Discovery Analytics at Virginia Tech, who helped me hone my skills in open source programming languages and made me realize that a BTech degree is equivalent to having a driving license.

I would like to express my heartfelt gratitude to my beautiful sister, Mahak and my handsome husband Ravi, for their care, humour, support, love and belief in my abilities. You both could see me when I could not see myself. Thanks a lot, guys.

A special thanks to all the people who took my courses at Udemy, joined my batches or one-to-one sessions, or met me through some corporate programs. Thank you so much for giving me this opportunity to coach you and learn this wonderful tool Selenium along with you.

Finally, I would like to express my heartfelt gratitude to the entire Selenium community from its creators to people who maintain the tool to everyone involved. Cheers to each one of you! It's a wonderful creation!

– *Pallavi Sharma*

Preface

Selenium is a test automation tool for web application functional testing that has gained significant popularity in the last decade or so. The reason for its popularity is that it is open source, it supports scripting in different programming languages like Java, C#, Python, Ruby, Perl, and JavaScript. It automates different browsers on different operating systems. No other tool in the market comes with this rich feature set with zero license cost. Many organizations big or small have moved towards Selenium. Also due to adaptation of Agile practices, CI/CD pipeline automation is no longer an option but a necessity.

Selenium implementation using Java as a programming language is widely used. In recent years, a significant rise is seen in the implementation of Selenium with Python, as this language has gained popularity. In this book, we will learn about the concepts of test automation using the tool Selenium, and implement them using the programming language Python.

Chapter1– In this chapter, introduces Selenium, the different components of Selenium, discusses why we should use Selenium and the Selenium architecture.

Chapter 2– In this chapter, discusses the Selenium IDE, its installation, how to create the first test for record and playback. It covers Selenium commands.

Chapter 3– In this chapter, talks about the concepts of the locators. Locators of Selenium allow us to identify the objects uniquely on the page so that we can perform actions on it.

Chapter 4– In this chapter,covers the setting system for writing our very first test using selenium webdriver on the eclipse IDE, using the PyDev plugin. It runsa test on Chrome, Firefox and the Internet Explorer browser.

Chapter 5– In this chapter, discusses the WebDriver, WebElements, and By classes of the selenium webdriver module of Python. It covers the different methods associated with these classes.

Chapter 6– In this chapter, discusses the unittest module. It is the unit test framework of the Python programming language. It also discusses its assertion module to help us assert our scripts.

Chapter 7– In this chapter, discuss the concept of synchronization. It covers static wait and dynamic wait.

Chapter 8– In this chapter, explains how we can parameterize our test using an external dataset like a csv file.

Chapter 9– In this chapter, discusses how Selenium automates different HTML elements. Form elements, tables, drop down.

Chapter 10– In this chapter, looks at some other HTML elements like frame, alerts and action class of Selenium

Chapter 11– In this chapter, discusses the concept of the page object model, which is a famous design pattern for Selenium test suite creations, which help manage object information.

Chapter 12– In this chapter, discusses how to implement the Selenium grid by invoking the Selenium server in the hub mode and node mode. It also covers how to make some changes in scripts to point it to the hub for execution.

Errata

We take immense pride in our work at BPB Publications and follow best practices to ensure the accuracy of our content to provide with an indulging reading experience to our subscribers. Our readers are our mirrors, and we use their inputs to reflect and improve upon human errors if any, occurred during the publishing processes involved. To let us maintain the quality and help us reach out to any readers who might be having difficulties due to any unforeseen errors, please write to us at :

errata@bpbonline.com

Your support, suggestions and feedbacks are highly appreciated by the BPB Publications' Family.

Table of Contents

CHAPTER 1
Introduction to Selenium

Software testing refers to a set of processes and procedures which help us identify whether the product at hand is getting built as per expectation or not. If we find any deviations we log them as defect, and in the subsequent releases we perform regression testing, retest the bugs, and eventually we are able to release a build to the market with an acceptable bug list. These regression tests, which we have to perform with every release cycle, are mandatory as well as monotonous in nature, which makes them an ideal candidate for test automation.

There are many tools available in the market which allows us to automate our web applications, both commercial and open source. We have tools like UFT, RFT, Silk, Watir, Selenium, and others. Of these, Selenium, which is an open source functional testing tool for web applications, is the most popular. In this chapter we will introduce it.

Structure

- History of Selenium
- Benefits of Selenium

- Components of Selenium
- Architecture of Selenium

Objective

In this chapter, we are going to learn about Selenium as a test automation tool--the reason for its popularity. We are also going to learn about the architecture of Selenium to understand how it executes tests on browsers.

History of Selenium

Selenium was created by *Jason Huggins*, while he was working at Thoughtworks in 2004. It was then called **JavaScriptTestRunner**. It was used to test an *internal time and expense application.* It was later released to the open source community as Selenium. It was named Selenium because it overcame the shortcomings of another competitor that was made by an organization Mercury. Selenium as a chemical is used to treat Mercury poisoning. The main website of Selenium is **http://seleniumhq.org/,** which is shown in the following screenshot. Here, you will find all the information related to the Selenium tool:

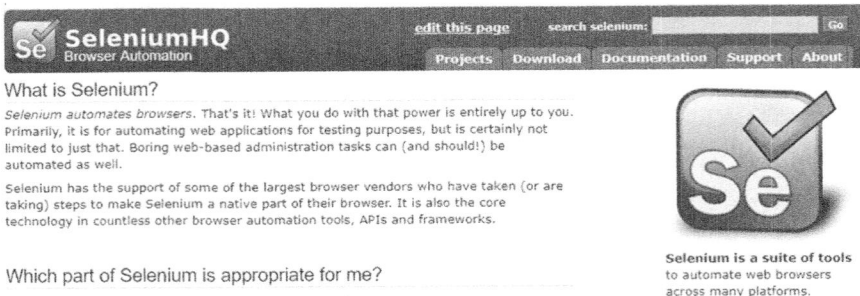

Figure 1.1

There are different tabs on this web page, let's have a look at what each represents:

- **Projects:** This tab basically lists the four projects, which make the Selenium tool. The Selenium IDE, Selenium RC, Selenium WebDriver, and Selenium Grid. We will talk in detail about these components in the coming chapters.
- **Download:** This tab, lists the various downloadthat are required while setting up our system for using the tool.

- **Documentation:** It provides detailed help that may be required to learn Selenium. It also provides code examples, in different programming languages, which Selenium supports. It is very well written, and should be a one-stop solution for all Selenium-related queries.

- **Support:** The support page provides information on chat, user groups, and the organization that is providing commercial support for the Selenium tool.

- **About:** The about section talks about news, events, history of Selenium and how one can get involved in the Selenium activities.

Benefits of Selenium

Selenium is one of the most popular open-source functional test automation tools for web applications. The reason for its popularity is due to the following:

- It supports multiple programming languages. You can code in Java, C#, Python, Ruby, and Perl.

- It supports automation of multiple browsers like IE, Firefox, Chrome, and Safari.

- It supports multiple operating systems like Windows, Mac, and Linux.

- It is available free of cost,

- It has a strong and active user community, which is very helpful.

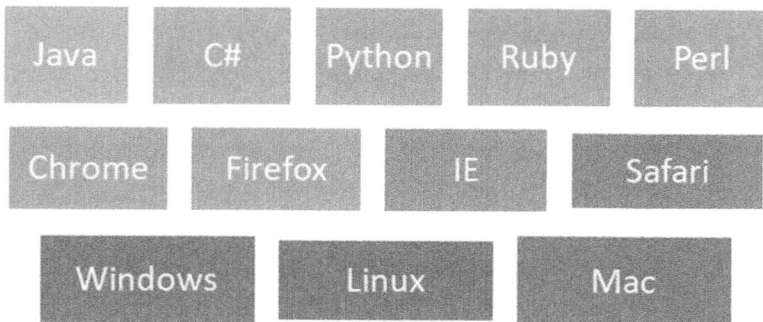

Figure 1.2

Components of Selenium

Selenium is not a one-test automation tool, but a group of four different tools, which are listed as follows, along with their usage:

- **Selenium IDE:** It is a tool used for recording and playing back scripts. It currently supports both Firefox and Chrome browsers. You can procure the tool from this link: **https://www.seleniumhq.org/selenium-ide/**

- **Selenium RC:** It was also known as Selenium 1.0. Although no longer supported, it was a combination of aSelenium server and a client, which allowed automation of any browser on any operating system.

- **SeleniumWebDriver:** Also known as Selenium 2.0, whose 3.0 version is now available. It uses the technology of WebDriver API, where every browser has the capability through its API to automate itself. Currently the Selenium versions are released through the WebDriver technique of browser automation.

- **Selenium Grid:** It uses server component from the Selenium RC, and executes it in two different modes as hub and node. This allows executions of multiple tests simultaneously, which saves time and cost.

Architecture of Selenium

The main component of Selenium which is used in projects for automation is the Selenium WebDriver. We are going to discuss its architecture, which has four main components, as follows:

- The client libraries available in different programming languages

- JSON wire protocol over HTTP for communication to send commands from client to server

- WebDriver for every browser

- **Browsers:** Chrome, Firefox, IE, Opera, and more

The following diagram shows the client libraries that are available in different programming languages. We create our scripts using them. These then send commands to the WebDriver server using the JSON wire protocol over HTTP. The WebDriver for each individual browser receives these commands and automates the browser, performing the action on them, thus achieving the task at hand:

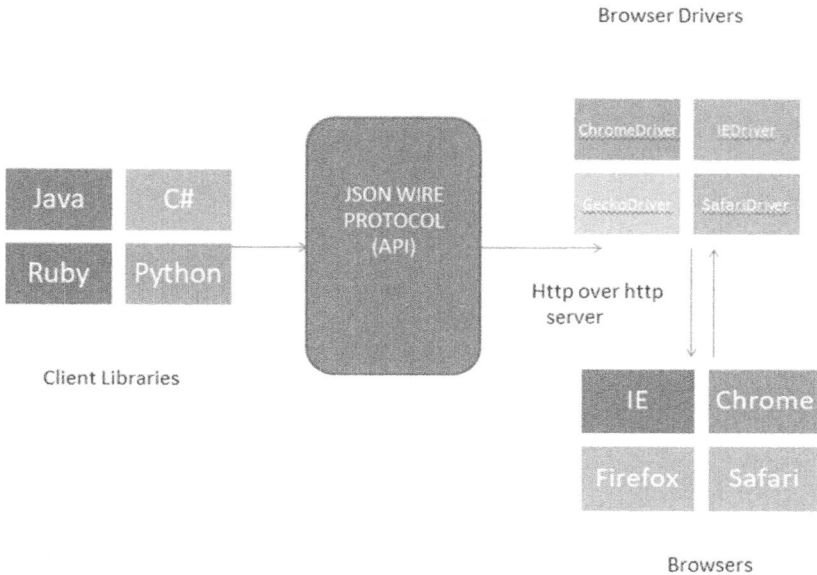

Figure 1.3

Conclusion

As we conclude this chapter, we understand the background of the test automation tool Selenium, its importance, and the reason behind its popularity in the test automation world. In our next chapter, we will be discussing a component of Selenium - the Selenium IDE.

Questions

1. Who created Selenium?
2. Which Selenium component is used for record and playback?
3. Why is Selenium popular?
4. Which protocol does Selenium WebDriver use for communication?
5. Is Selenium 1.0 still in use?

CHAPTER 2
Selenium IDE

In this chapter, we will discussthe Selenium IDE component. This component allows us to record and playback our tests. It is an integral component of the Selenium project, and has been recently upgraded and brought back into function with the help of the organization **Applitools**.

Selenium IDE, also known as SIDE stands for Selenium Integrated Development Environment. It is one of the four projects of the Selenium ecosystem. The earlier version of Selenium IDE worked only on the Firefox browser. But the changes in the Firefox browser from version 55 didn't allow Selenium IDE integration. At this juncture, Applitools helped Selenium community with a group of dedicated engineers **(https://github.com/seleniumHQ/selenium-ide/graphs/contributors)** and brought back Selenium IDE. The current version supports both Firefox and Chrome browsers.

Structure

- Installing Selenium IDE
- Walk through of the demo application

- Creating our first test
- Selenium IDE commands

Objective

The Selenium IDE component is used to record and play back tests. The current version, which supports both Firefox and Chrome browsers, has a rich feature list. It now allows running tests in parallel, supports JavaScript execution, allows usage of if conditions and many such cool things. To know more about it, read the article available here:

https://applitools.com/blog/why-Selenium-ide-2019?utm_ referrer=https://www.google.com/

Installation of Selenium IDE

To install Selenium IDE, we have to follow the below-mentioned instructions:

1. Open the Chrome browser and follow this link:

   https://www.seleniumhq.org/selenium-ide/

2. Here, we need to select the choice, Chrome or Firefox download.

3. It will open a new browser window, with the option asking **Add to Chrome** as shown in the following screenshot:

Figure 2.1

4. You need to select it.

5. It will launch a popup, asking permission. Select **Add extension** as shown in the following screenshot:

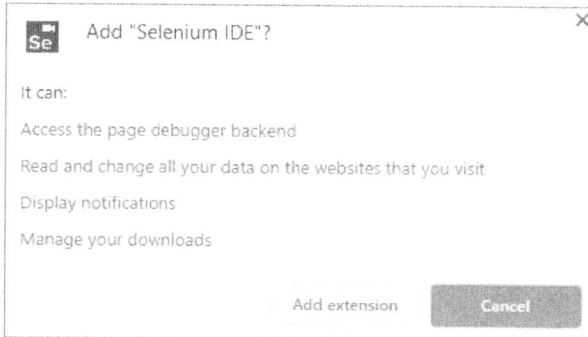

Figure 2.2

6. You will now be able to see Selenium IDE icon in your browser menu bar.

After installing the Selenium IDE, we need to have a look at a demo web application. We will need this application to understand a few concepts of test automation using Selenium. So let us get introduced to it.

Introduction to demo web application

We will consider a demo web application, which is an ecommerce website. As we learn the concepts of test automation with Selenium using Python as a programming language, we will use functional flows from the web application. We will also look at a few other web applications as we learn to handle some specific html elements and deal with some specific scenarios.

The URL of the demo application is: **http://practice.bpbonline.com/catalog/index.php**

As you follow the URL, you will see the following screen:

Welcome to BPBOnline

Welcome Guest! Would you like to log yourself in? Or would you prefer to create an account?

New Products For April

Fire Down Below $29.99	Microsoft Internet Keyboard PS/2 $69.99	The Wheel Of Time $99.99
Courage Under Fire $29.99	Matrox G400 32MB $499.99	SWAT 3: Close Quarters Battle $79.99
You've Got Mail $34.99	A Bug's Life $35.99	Hewlett Packard LaserJet 1100Xi $499.99

Figure 2.3

Following are some of the specific functional flows in the application:

- Register the user
- Login and logout of user
- Change profile of user
- Change password of user
- Buy product
- Search product

From the previous list of application business scenarios, we will take the login-logout business scenario as a sample one for our first record and playback script in Selenium IDE. Record script basically means with the help of Selenium IDE, we will capture the user actions as we perform the steps to login and then logout from the application. These will be captured by the Selenium IDE, as commands. It will then be played back, where Selenium IDE will launch the browser and will be able to perform the exact steps to login and logout of the application without any user intervention.

Let's perform the following steps for login–logout:

1. Open the application using the URL: **http://practice. bpbonline.com/catalog/index.php**

2. Click on the **My Account** link.

3. Fill in the user details; you can use the following user credentials:

    *   Username: bpb@bpb.com

    *   Password: bpb@123

    Or you can also create your own account, by registering yourself and then using those credentials.

4. Click on the **Sign in** button

5. Click on the **Log Off** link

6. Click on the **Continue** link

Please note the above scenario is not a test case, as we have added no steps for the validation. There are only test steps.

Record and playback in Selenium IDE

The following are the steps we need to perform for recording and playing back in Selenium IDE:

1. Open Chrome browser.

2. On it, click on the **Selenium IDE** icon. It will popup Selenium IDE window as shown in the following screenshot:

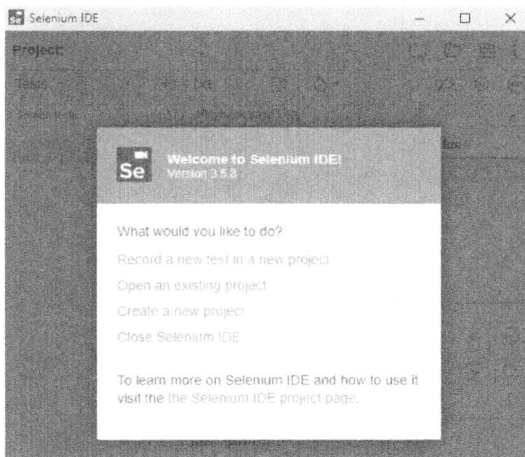

Figure 2.4

3. Here, we will select **Record a new test in a new project**.

4. Provide a project name in the next screen.

5. Then in the next screen, provide the base URL for recording:

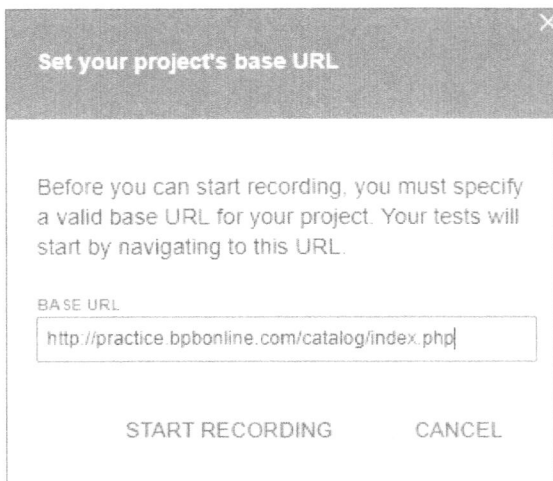

Figure 2.5

6. Click here on **START RECORDING**.

7. This will launch the browser with the application URL, and a message **Selenium IDE is recording....** Now, whatever steps we perform on the browser, they will all be captured by the IDE. Check the following screenshot:

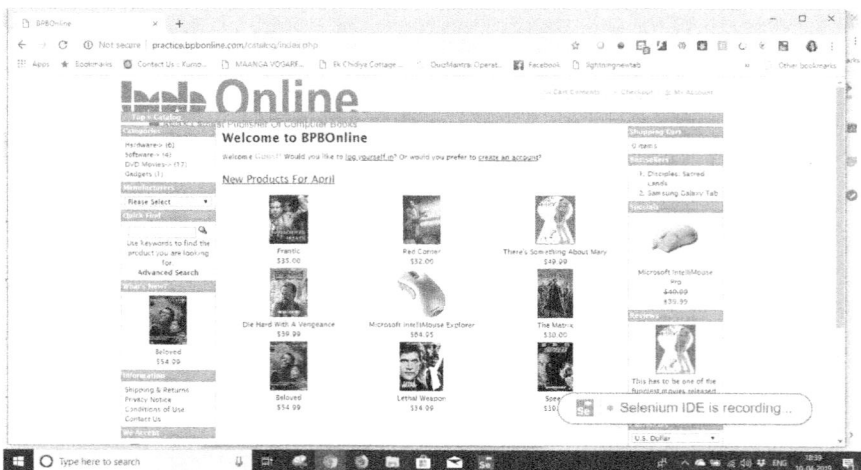

Figure 2.6

7. After performing all the steps, close the browser, and on the Selenium IDE, click the ⊛ (stop button).
8. Provide a name to the test, and save the project at a location in your system.
9. After the login logout steps are captured, your test should look as follows:

http://practice.bpbonline.com		
Command	Target	Value
1 open	/catalog/index.php	
2 click	id=tdb3	
3 type	name=email_address	bpb@bpb.com
4 type	name=password	bpb@123
5 click	xpath=//button[@id='tdb1']/span	
6 click	css=#tdb4 > .ui-button-text	
7 click	css=#tdb4 > .ui-button-text	

Figure 2.7

It could be possible that Selenium IDE may capture some other locator value for the same object which you see in the target field, which is absolutely fine, as long as you are able to replay the test successfully.

There could be some other extra steps captured as Selenium IDE captures every mouse action, we need to delete those extra steps and only have those steps that match our manual action.

Structure of Selenium IDE Test

If we look at the above image, there are three columns which form a Selenium IDE test:

- **Command**, which provides information of the action being performed.
- **Target**, which talks about the object on which the action is to be performed.
- **Value**, which talks about the data which will be used in the test.

The commands of Selenium IDE fall under three categories, as follows:

- **Action**: Those commands, which change the state of the application.
- **Assertion**: Those commands which verify the state of the application after it is performed. There are two types of assertion commands that are as follows:
  - o **Verify:** These commands, if they fail, still allow execution of the next step in the test case.
  - o **Assert:** These commands, if they fail, don't allow the execution of the next step in the test case.
- **Accessor:** Those commands which allow storage of value, or creation of variables to be used in the test.

Let us write the login-logout scenario, this time with the validation steps:

1. Open the application.
2. Click **My Account** link.
3. Type the **E-mail address** and **Password**.
4. Click the **Sign In** button.
5. Verify **My Account Information** text on the screen.
6. Click on the **Log Off** link.
7. Click on the **Continue** link.
8. Verify **Welcome to BPB Online** text on the screen.

   To record the above scenario, we will perform the same steps as we did for the login-logout one, except for steps 5 and 8, where we will performthe following.

9. Add the **Command** verify text during the recording, after you have logged in. Refer to the following screenshot:

	-text	
9	*verify text*	

Command	verify text|	▾
Target	verify text	
Value	verify title	

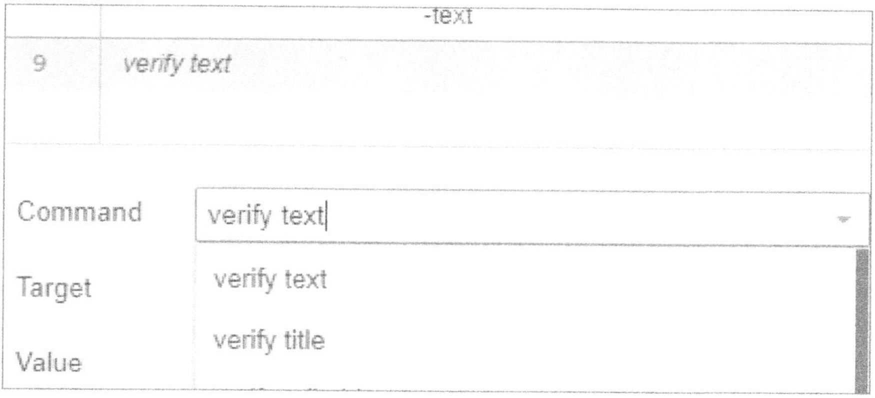

Figure 2.8

10. Now we will select the **Target** for that we click on the icon ⬚ , and highlight and click the element, whose text we need to capture for verification. Refer to the following screenshot:

My Account Information

Figure 2.9

11. We copy the text from here and put it in the **Value** field. So finally, our command would look like the following:

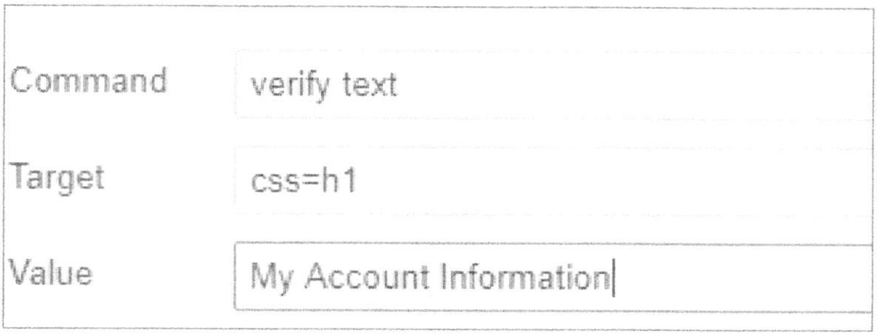

Command	verify text
Target	css=h1
Value	My Account Information|

Figure 2.10

12. We will perform a similar action for step 8.

13. Complete the steps of recording, and save the test for playback. As you playback the test, you will see all the steps

in green. Now let us try to see the action of failure by changing the text of My Account Information to Junk. We will find out that although the test gets executed, but reports failure on the verification step. The following screenshot shows the behavior:

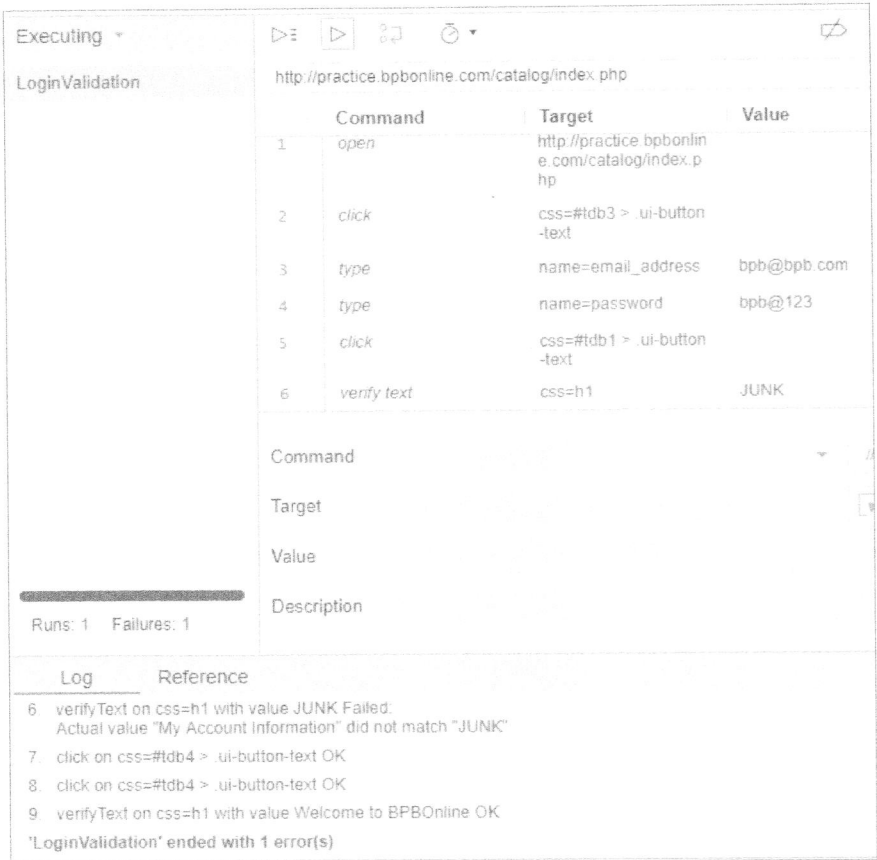

	Command	Target	Value
1	open	http://practice.bpbonline.com/catalog/index.php	
2	click	css=#tdb3 > .ui-button -text	
3	type	name=email_address	bpb@bpb.com
4	type	name=password	bpb@123
5	click	css=#tdb1 > .ui-button -text	
6	verify text	css=h1	JUNK

Command

Target

Value

Description

Runs: 1   Failures: 1

Log   Reference

6. verifyText on css=h1 with value JUNK Failed:
    Actual value "My Account Information" did not match "JUNK"

7. click on css=#tdb4 > .ui-button-text OK

8. click on css=#tdb4 > .ui-button-text OK

9. verifyText on css=h1 with value Welcome to BPBOnline OK

'LoginValidation' ended with 1 error(s)

Figure 2.11

14. Now, for the same test, if we change the **Command** from verify text, to assert text we will see that the execution will get halted at the step of failure. This is shown as follows:

	Command	Target	Value
2	click	css=#tdb3 > .ui-button-text	
3	type	name=email_address	bpb@bpb.com
4	type	name=password	bpb@123
5	click	css=#tdb1 > .ui-button-text	
6	assert text	css=h1	JUNK
7	click	css=#tdb4 > .ui-button-text	

LoginValidation* http://practice.bpbonline.com/catalog/index.php

Command

Target

Value

Description

Runs: 1   Failures: 1

Log   Reference

3. type on name=email_address with value bpb@bpb.com OK
4. type on name=password with value bpb@123 OK
5. click on css=#tdb1 > .ui-button-text OK
6. assertText on css=h1 with value JUNK Failed:
   Actual value "My Account Information" did not match "JUNK"
'LoginValidation' ended with 1 error(s)

Figure 2.12

So there are three states of execution here:
- **Green:** All pass
- **Red:** Fail
- **White:** Not executed

Conclusion

In thischapter, we discussed about the Selenium IDE component. We saw how we could use it for recording and playing back tests. We could use Selenium IDE for proofing concepts, to see if our application supports Selenium or not. Sometimes we struggle to find a locator for an object,in such cases recording the scenario in Selenium IDE is also helpful.

In our next chapter we will discuss the concept of locators, what techniques Selenium uses to recognize objects on web application.

Questions

1. What browsers Selenium IDE supports?

2. What does SIDE stands for?

3. Explain the difference between `verify` and `assert` command?

CHAPTER 3

Locators in Selenium

Introduction

When we try to automate a web application, there are two important steps to consider. One is to identify the object uniquely on which we would want to perform the action. The second is to perform the action on the identified object. To identify the object uniquely on the web page, Selenium provides us with some locator strategies. In this chapter we will discuss and explore them.

Structure

- What is a locator?
- Different types of locators
- Where are locators used?

Objective

When working with open source technology like Selenium, it is crucial for us to understand that as end user what strategy Selenium uses to identify an object on a page. As we are going to write scripts to automate applications at hand, we will have to provide object information using one of the locator strategies which Selenium will use to identify the object on the page so that the required action can be performed on it.

What is a locator?

Locator is a technique to identify the object on a page uniquely by using different identification methods. Once the object is identified, the action can be performed on it. Selenium provides us with the following locator techniques to identify the object on the page:

- ID
- NAME
- XPATH
- CSS
- DOM
- LINKTEXT
- PARTIALLINKTEXT

To understand the different strategies of the locators, which Selenium uses to identify the object on the page, we will take the example of an HTML code snippet from our web application: **http://practice. bpbonline.com/catalog/index.php** my account page, which we see, when we click the **My Account** link of the home page. The idea is to explore the HTML code associated with **E-mail Address** field, **Password** field, and the **Sign In** button. So let us have a look at it:

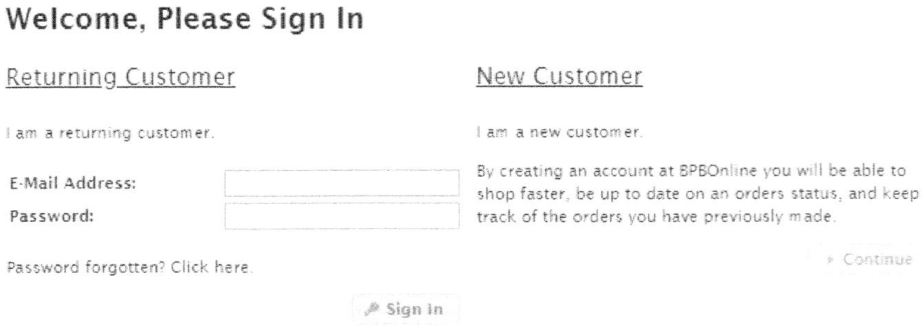

Welcome, Please Sign In

Returning Customer   New Customer

I am a returning customer.   I am a new customer.

E-Mail Address: By creating an account at BPBOnline you will be able to
                                                    shop faster, be up to date on an orders status, and keep
Password: track of the orders you have previously made.

Password forgotten? Click here.   ▶ Continue

                          ⚲ Sign In

Figure 3.1

If we right click the HTML page, and select **View page source**. Refer to the following screenshot:

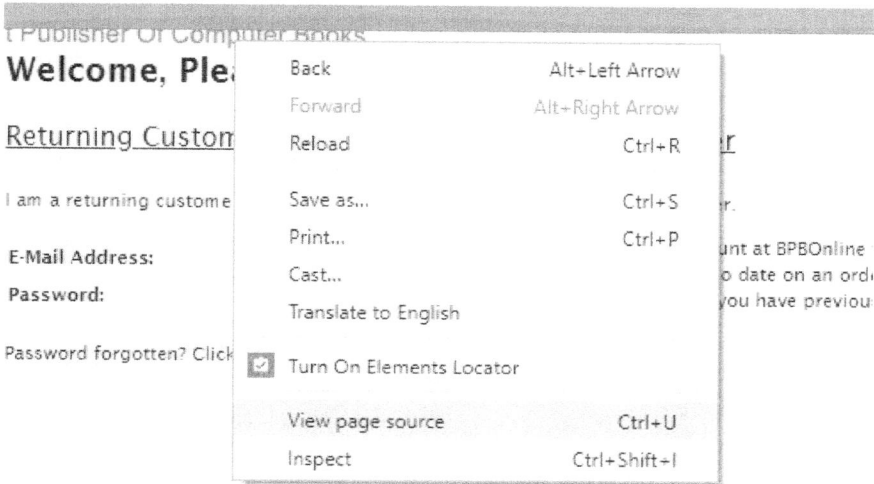

Figure 3.2

We can see the HTML content associated with the web page. It is displayed as follows:

Figure 3.3

As we have seen, the above HTML content is associated with three objects – username and password fields, and sign in button, let us try to understand the different locator strategies Selenium can use to identify them so that an action can be performed on them as our automation script executes. So, the following is explained below:

- **ID:** The ID locator is fetched from the ID attribute of an HTML element. If the HTML element of interest has an ID attribute, we use it to identify the object uniquely. The example of this is the **Sign In** button, which has the `id = tdb1`:`<button id="tdb1" type="submit">Sign In</button>`

- **NAME:** This attribute is fetched from the NAME attribute of the HTML element. The data associated with this property of the HTML element is used to identify the object uniquely on the web page. Examples of this property areusername, and password fields:

  ```
  <input type="text" name="email_address" />
  <input type="password" name="password" maxlength="40" />
  ```

- **XPATH:** The path traversed to reach the node of interest in an XML document is known as **XPATH**. To create the XPATH locator for an element, we look at an HTML document as if it is an XML document, and then traverse the path to reach it. The XPATH can either be a relative or an absolute one:

  o A relative XPATH will be in relation to a landmark node. A node which has a strong identifier like an ID or NAME. It uses `//` in its path creation. Example: `//input[@name="email_address"]`

  o An absolute XPATH starts from the root node HTML. It uses a single slash `/`. It is more prone to changes if the document structure undergoes changes during the development of the application, so it is generally avoided.

  Example:`/HTML/body/div[2]/form[0]/table/tbody/tr[2]/input`

- **CSS:** It stands for Cascading Style Sheets. We can use this as well to identify the objects uniquely on the web page. The syntax is as follows:

  o If the HTML of the object has an ID attribute then, `css=#ID`, for example, `css=#tdb1`

  o Else, `css=HTMLtag[prop=value]`, for example, `css=input[name='email_address']`

- **DOM:** It stands for Document Object Model. It allows object identification by using the HTML tag name associated with the object.

- **LINKTEXT:** Generally, whenever we encounter a link in the application we can use it to identify the object on the page. For example the **My Account** link can be identified using the same link text as seen in the web page

- **PARTIAL LINK TEXT:** We can also use a sub part of a complete text of the link to identify it on the web page and then perform actions on it.

It is important to use an appropriate locator to identify the object on the page, which is unique, helps in quick identification of object and is robust to application changes during the development process. Generally, if the object HTML has IDor NAME we use it to identify the object on the page. Then we use XPATH, followed by CSS and the last option is DOM. If it is a link, we always use LINKTEXT or PARTIAL LINK TEXT to identify the element on the page. So ideally, this should be the approach we need to take.

Conclusion

In this chapter we discussed the concept of locators; we understood its various types. We also saw where and how they would be needed. These locator strategies are standard in Selenium. They are not going to get modified in any version, and have been consistent from old versions as well. Lastly, we need to keep in mind that the locator strategy we are choosing to identify the object has to be robust, and help to locate the object quickly on the page. In the next chapter we will learn the steps to setup Selenium and Eclipse IDE on Windows OS.

Questions

1. What are the different locator strategies used in Selenium?
2. Where can we find ID and NAME locators?
3. What is the difference between relative and absolute XPATH locator?
4. Create CSS locator for an object which has ID property available.
5. How will you recognize a link in Selenium?

CHAPTER 4
Installation and Setup

In this chapter we will learn how to prepare our system with the required software so that we are able to write our test automation scripts and execute them. We will need to have Python, Java Runtime Engine (JRE), Eclipse IDE, PyDev. After setting upthesesoftware for creating scripts, we will need to set up Selenium in the system, and download the browser drivers for execution on the individual drivers.

Structure

- Installation and setting up
- Installing Selenium Pythonmodule
- Installing JRE
- Installing Eclipse IDE
- Setting up PyDev
- Installing different drivers for Chrome, Firefox, and IE browser
- Running the very first program on three browsers

Objective

This chapter will help us to understand the steps to setup Selenium and Eclipse IDE on Windows system

Installation and setting up

Before we start to learn writing scripts to automate browser using Selenium WebDriver, we have to prepare our system with a few software. We will require the following:

- **Python setup: https://www.python.org/downloads/** [download the latest version] [3.7]
- **Java JRE: https://www.oracle.com/technetwork/Java/Javase/ downloads/jre8-downloads-2133155.html,** and install it on the system.
- **Eclipse IDE: https://www.eclipse.org/downloads/**

After we have installed and setup the above software in our system, we need to install PyDev in the Eclipse environment. To setup PyDev in the Eclipse environment, we have to perform the following actions:

1. Open Eclipse.
2. Click on `Help | Install New Software`.
3. Provide in there, URL: **http://pydev.org/updates**

The following screenshot shows the same:

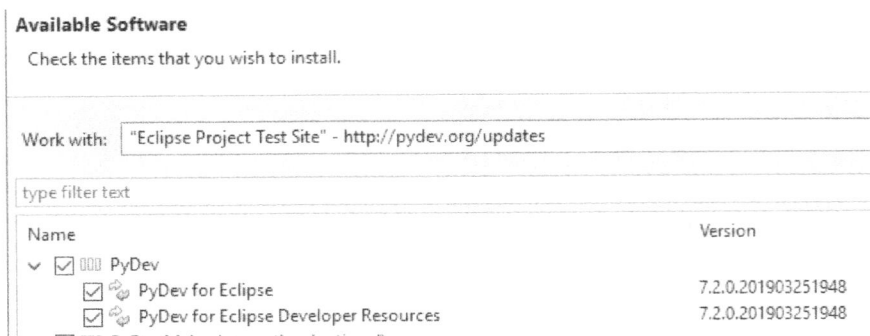

Available Software

Check the items that you wish to install.

Work with: "Eclipse Project Test Site" - http://pydev.org/updates

type filter text

Name	Version
☑ ▢▢▢ PyDev	
☑ 🔖 PyDev for Eclipse	7.2.0.201903251948
☑ 🔖 PyDev for Eclipse Developer Resources	7.2.0.201903251948

Figure 4.1

4. Allow installation of PyDev plugin.

Now the Eclipse environment is ready to create Python projects, and understand Python syntax as well. The next step is to install the Selenium Python module.

Installing Selenium Python module

The modules of Python are available on the website **(http://www. pypi.org)**. From here, we will search the module for Selenium and use the `pipinstall` command.

1. Open the URL: **https://pypi.org/project/selenium/**

   The above URL provides information about the Selenium module of Python, the command to install it, and the documentation available with it.

2. To install the module, open the Command Prompt and type `pip install selenium`, shown as follows:

Command Prompt

```
Microsoft Windows [Version 10.0.17134.706]
(c) 2018 Microsoft Corporation. All rights reserved.

C:\Users\write>pip install selenium
```

Figure 4.2

3. The preceding command will install the Selenium Python module, and the environment will now be ready to accept Selenium commands to automate the browser.

Creating Python project in Eclipse

We will now perform the steps to create a Python project in Eclipse, and write down our first script to open the browser with the URL of our demosite application and close it. We will perform it for all three browsers: Internet Explorer, Firefox, and Chrome.

Let's see in a step-by-step manner:

1. Go to **File | Create New Project**. In that window, select **PyDev** project. Refer to the following screenshot:

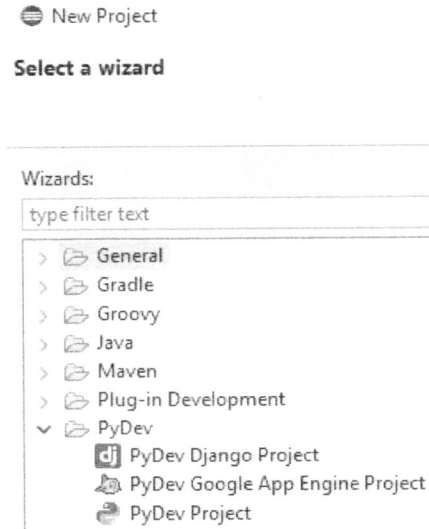

⊕ New Project

Select a wizard

Wizards:

> type filter text

> 📁 General
> 📁 Gradle
> 📁 Groovy
> 📁 Java
> 📁 Maven
> 📁 Plug-in Development
∨ 📁 PyDev
　　🗐 PyDev Django Project
　　🗺 PyDev Google App Engine Project
　　🐍 PyDev Project

Figure 4.3

2. Provide name to the project, select **Python** interpreter, it is advisable to choose **Quick Auto Config**. Refer to the following screenshot:

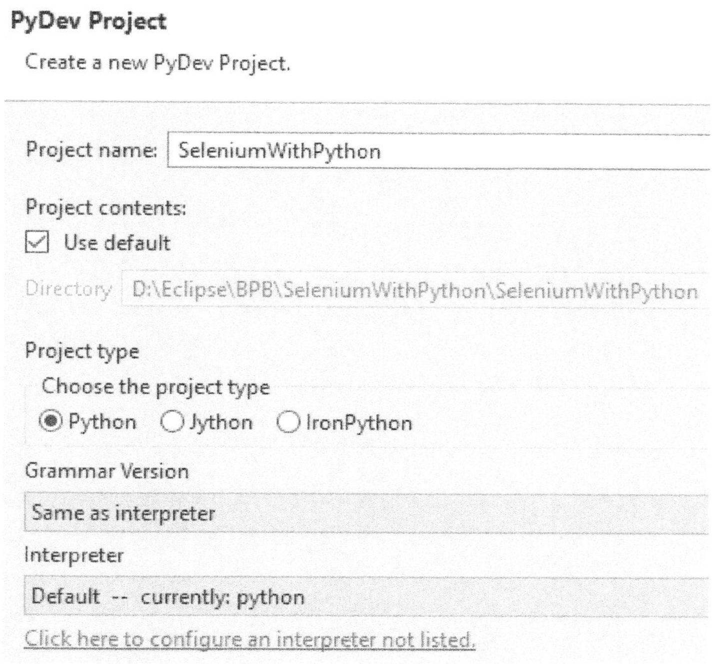

PyDev Project

Create a new PyDev Project.

Project name: | SeleniumWithPython

Project contents:
☑ Use default

Directory | D:\Eclipse\BPB\SeleniumWithPython\SeleniumWithPython

Project type
  Choose the project type
  ◉ Python ○ Jython ○ IronPython

Grammar Version

Same as interpreter

Interpreter

Default -- currently: python

Click here to configure an interpreter not listed.

Figure 4.4

3. Click on **Next**, and then `Finish`. Eclipse may ask you to open the Python perspective, select **Yes**.

We are now ready to write down scripts in Python to automate the browsers.

Automating Chrome browser

To automate the Chrome browser, we first need to download the Chrome driver. Depending on the Chrome browser version we have on our system, and the operating system we are using, we need to download the suitable driver. It is advisable to ensure that you have the latest version of the browser.

1. To download Chrome driver, visit the link:

   http://chromedriver.chromium.org/downloads

2. Drivers are available as per the operating system type for download:

Index of /74.0.3729.6/

Name	Last modified
Parent Directory	
chromedriver_linux64.zip	2019-03-12 19:25:26
chromedriver_mac64.zip	2019-03-12 19:25:27
chromedriver_win32.zip	2019-03-12 19:25:29
notes.txt	2019-03-14 18:17:49

Figure 4.5

3. Here, we are taking an example of the win32 system. So we download the win32 ChromedriverZIP folder, and extract the .exe file from it.

4. In Eclipse, where we create our project, we create a folder there, called as drivers. We copy this chrome driver .exe file into that folder. So finally our project would look as follows:

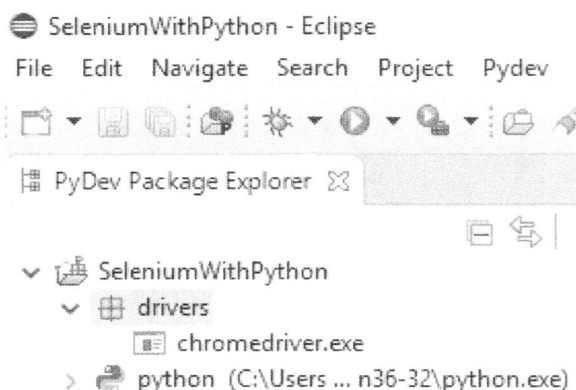

Figure 4.6

Writing the first script

We will now write our very first script to automate the Chrome browser, where we will launch the browser, open the application, and then close the browser.

Refer to the following script:

```
from selenium import webdriver

browser =webdriver.Chrome(executable_path='D:\Eclipse\BPB\SeleniumWithPython\SeleniumWithPython\drivers\chromedriver.exe')
browser.get('http://practice.bpbonline.com/catalog/index.php')
browser.quit()
```

Figure 4.7

Let us understand the above script. The first statement from `Selenium import webdriver` will import Selenium classes in the file. This will allow usage of the Selenium commands in the script. So basically, we can create object of WebDriver, and call different methods associated with it to handle the browser. It will fail if Selenium module is not imported. The next statement initializes the browser objectby creating an instance of the Chrome object and passing the path of the executable driver. With the Selenium WebDriver, every browser requires their own WebDriver to automate them.

The get methodallows the browser to be launched with the URL that has been provided, and the quit method closes all the instances of the browser opened from this script.

Automating Firefox browser

To automate the Firefox browser, we need to download the `geckodriver`. The `geckodriver` is the APIwhich allows us to automate the Firefox browser. It acts as a bridge between Selenium and the browser. Here as well, we need to select the driver version based on the operating system and the Firefox version. To download the driver, we need to visit the link: **https://github.com/mozilla/geckodriver/releases**

Select the driver according to your system; here we select for win64 from the following list:

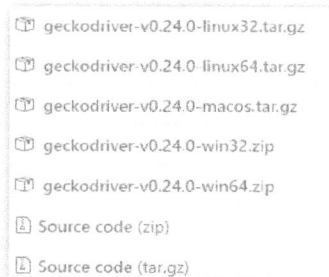

Figure 4.8

Once we download the `geckodriver` for win64, we extract the `geckodriver.exe` file from the ZIPfolder and put it in the `drivers` folder in the Python project of Eclipse. Now we are ready to create the script which will open the application on Firefox browser and close it:

```
from selenium import webdriver

browser =webdriver.Chrome(executable_path=r'D:\Eclipse\BPB\SeleniumWithPython\SeleniumWithPython\drivers\chromedriver.exe')
browser.get('http://practice.bpbonline.com/catalog/index.php')
browser.quit()
```

Figure 4.9

Automating Internet Explorer

To automate the Internet Explorer browser, we have to download the `IEdriverserver.exe` file. This file is available on the **https://www.seleniumhq.org/download/** website.

The Internet Explorer Driver Server

This is required if you want to make use of the latest and greatest features of the WebDriver InternetExplorerDriver. Please make sure that this is available on your $PATH (or %PATH% on Windows) in order for the IE Driver to work as expected.

Download version 3.14.0 for (recommended) 32 bit Windows IE or 64 bit Windows IE CHANGELOG

Figure 4.10

Depending upon the operating systemwe are using, we will download that particular IE driver. Once the `.exe` file is downloaded, we will save it in the `drivers` folder of our project, and write the following script to open the application in the IE browser:

```
from selenium import webdriver

browser =webdriver.Ie(executable_path=r'D:\Eclipse\SeleniumWithPython\drivers\iedriverserver.exe')
browser.get('http://5elementslearning.com/demosite')
browser.quit()
```

Figure 4.11

Conclusion

So, in this chapter we have learned how to set up our system, create project and automate the three browsers. The official documentation of Selenium Python bindings is available here: **https://seleniumhq. github.io/selenium/docs/api/py/index.html**

Now our system in ready to for us to write down our Selenium tests for the multi-browser support available with Python programming languages, aiding the manual testers by automation and reducing the workload. In our next chapter we will learn how to work with different types of WebElements, understand the concept of synchronization, and parameterization, which forms the basic building blocks for automation.

Questions

1. Why do we have to import WebDriver module to write Selenium scripts?
2. What is `geckodriver` used for?
3. Can Selenium automate IE browser?

CHAPTER 5

Understanding WebDriver, WebElement, and By

In this chapter, we will introduce the entities **WebDriver, WebElement,** and **By** of Selenium module. The WebDriver refers to the browser object. The WebElement refers to the HTMLelements on the page. The By helps us create the locator objects on the page. So let us understand how are they used, and what all methods are associated with them.

Structure

- WebDriver
- WebElement
- By

Objective

The Selenium module of Python programming language contains three crucial entities--WebDriver, WebElement, and By. The WebDriver helps us automate the browser object and has methods for it. The WebElement helps us automate the HTML element on the page, and has methods to perform action on them. The By class helps us locate object using different locator strategies supported by Selenium, like ID, name, XPATH, and others.

Introduction to Selenium module

The Selenium module in Python contains three important entities, WebDriver, WebElement, and By. In the following table it shows us the relation of these entities with our objects of automation

The following table shows their relation to the web entity:

WebDriver	Browser
WebElement	HTML element
By	Locator to identify the element on page

Table 5.1: *Relation between Selenium module and web entities*

Let us understand these entities in more detail.

WebDriver

The WebDriver object refers to the browser. It controls the browser by sending commands to the browser via the **JSONWireProtocol**. The details of this protocol are available here: **https://github.com/SeleniumHQ/Selenium/wiki/JsonWireProtocol.** Any implementation of WebDriver for automating any browser will have to abide by this. Let us have a look at the few methods available which help in browser actions:

Methods	Description
`get(url)`	Opens a web page with the given URL.
`findElement(By)`	This method takes a By object as argument, and finds the object on the web page which matches that locator. It returns the first found match. In Python we have `find_element_by_id`, `find_element_by_name`, `find_element_by_xpath` methods to locate elements.
`findElements(By)`	This method returns a list of all elements which match the locator value provided by the By object on the web page.
`forward()`	This command will take you to the next page.

back()	This command will take you to the previous page.
page_source	This command will return the entire HTML content of the page.
Title	Returns the current title of the page.
current_url	Returns the current URL of the page.
Close	Close the current instance of the browser.
Quit	Close the current instance of the browser and all the associated windows.

Table 5.2: Methods available in WebDriver

WebElement

The WebElement object refers to the HTML element on the web page. All methods that interact with the DOM will work through this interface. Before the implementation of any method, it does a freshness check to ensure if the element is still valid, and only then it acts. If the element reference is not valid it throws StaleElementReferenceException. Let us have a look at some of the methods available with this interface:

Methods	Actions
click()	It performs click operation on a web element.
clear()	It performs a clear operation on a web element.
get_attribute()	This method returns the data associated with the property of the HTML element at the time of execution. For example, you can fetch the href attribute with an anchor element.
is_displayed()	Returns true, if the element is visible to the user.
is_enabled()	Returns true, if the element is enabled.
is_selected()	Returns true, if the element is selected, for example, a radio button is selected.
send_keys()	It allows typing of text on an element, generally a textbox.
Text	It fetches the text associated with the HTML element.

Table 5.3: Methods available in WebElements

By

The By class of Selenium allows us to locate the web element on the page. It uses the following strategies:

- ID
- NAME
- XPATH
- CSS_SELECTOR
- TAG_NAME
- LINK_TEXT
- PARTIAL_LINK_TEXT
- CLASS_NAME

To locate the element on a web page we use the find_element_by_* method, where the * replaces any of the preceding locatorstrategy to find the element on the web page.

Now let us try to write down the script for the scenario of login-logout using the methods we have learnt above for these entities. The steps for the login-logout for our application are as follows:

1. Open the application with URL: **http://practice.bpbonline.com/catalog/index.php**
2. Click on **My Account** link.
3. Type email address and password.
4. Click **Sign In** button.
5. Click **Log Off** link.
6. Click **Continue** link.

We have learnt in earlier chapters that a link is to be identified by its link text which we see on the screen. To identify the username, we can use the name property having the value **email_address**, the password field has the name property **password**, and the sign in button has an id property **tdb1**, as you can see in the HTML of its page:

```
<table border="0" cellspacing="0" cellpadding="2" width="100%">
  <tr>
    <td class="fieldKey">E-Mail Address:</td>
    <td class="fieldValue"><input type="text" name="email_address" /></td>
  </tr>
  <tr>
    <td class="fieldKey">Password:</td>
    <td class="fieldValue"><input type="password" name="password" maxlength="40" /></td>
  </tr>
</table>

<p><a href="http://practice.bpbonline.com/catalog/password_forgotten.php">Password forgotten? Click here.</a></p>

<p align="right"><span class="tdbLink"><button id="tdb1" type="submit">Sign In</button></span><script
```

Figure 5.1

Let us now write the steps to automate the above scenario.

So in the following code, we are clicking on the **MyAccount** link, then typing the email address and password. Then we click on the **Sign In** button, and if our credentials are valid we should be able to login to the application. Then we click on the **Log Off** link, and click on the **Continue** link to complete the process.

```
from selenium import webdriver

browser =webdriver.Chrome(executable_path=r'D:\Eclipse\BPB\SeleniumWithPython\SeleniumWithPython\drivers\chromedriver.exe')
browser.get('http://practice.bpbonline.com/catalog/index.php')
browser.find_element_by_link_text("My Account").click()
browser.find_element_by_name("email_address").send_keys("bpb@bpb.com")
browser.find_element_by_name("password").send_keys("bpb@123")
browser.find_element_by_id("tdb1").click()
browser.find_element_by_link_text("Log Off").click()
browser.find_element_by_link_text("Continue").click()
browser.quit()
```

Figure 5.2

Conclusion

In this chapter, we learnt how Selenium WebDriver helps automate the browser, identify the element on a web page and perform actions on it. The above test script can be executed on Firefox and Internet Explorer browsers by changing the executable path to their respective WebDrivers. The rest of the test script looks exactly the same. We understood the different methods associated with the WebDriver object, WebElement object and the By locator object, which allows objects to be identified using different locator strategies.

In the next chapter, we will see how we can structure our Selenium scripts using **PyUnit** tests. We will study the **unittest** framework, which has derived its features from the **JUnit** and **NUnit** framework.

Questions
1. How will you close all open windows for a browser object?
2. What is the difference between findelement and findelements method?
3. What are the different locator strategies available for By class?

CHAPTER 6
Unittest in Python

Most of the high level programming languages have a unit test framework associated with them. Like Java has JUnit, .Net has NUnit. Similarly Python has PyUnit or unittest associated with it. It was created by *Kent Beck* and *Erich Gamma*. The unittest framework supports test automation, with the help of text fixtures. We will learn more about it in this chapter.

Structure

- What is unittest?
- Structure of unittest
- Writing first unittest
- Adding assertions in the test

Objective

When we are writing our test scripts, it is important that we structure them with the help of a unittest framework. The Python programming language makes available unittest, which is the unit test framework.

In this chapter, we will understand how we use it to structure our code and write scripts with.

The unitest and its structure

The unittest is the unit testing framework in Python. Its features are inspired from JUnit, which is a unit testing framework for Java programming language. Applying a unit testing framework at the code level helps us introduce structure to our code. It also ensures that we can add assertions in the test code, which we require as we are writing test automation scripts.

In a general unittest test case, the class which we create is derived from `unittest.TestCase`. We can have a `setUp()` and a `tearDown()` method there. In the `setUp()` method, we generally write code which helps in preparing the system, and test environment. And in the `tearDown()` method, we write scripts to clean up the environment. In between these methods we have our functions which is where the code to actually test is created. These functions are written using the `test_` prefix. We then execute the tests by calling `unittest.main()` method at the end of the file.

A unittest contains the following important entities:
- **Test fixture:** It expresses the process to execute test, followed by clean up action.
- **Test case:** It is the basic unit of testing.
- **Test suite:** It is a collection of test cases.
- **Test runner:** A test runner manages the execution of the test and presents the result to the user.

Let us see an example of script for login logout, where we will be applying unittest:

```
from selenium import webdriver
import unittest

class Login(unittest.TestCase):
    def setUp(self):
        self.driver =webdriver.Chrome(executable_path=r'D:\Eclipse\BPB\SeleniumWithPython\SeleniumWithPython\drivers\chromedriver.exe')
        self.base_url = "http://practice.bpbonline.com/catalog/index.php"

    def test_login(self):
        driver = self.driver
        driver.get(self.base_url)
        driver.find_element_by_link_text("My Account").click()
        driver.find_element_by_name("email_address").clear()
        driver.find_element_by_name("email_address").send_keys("bpb@pb.com")
        driver.find_element_by_name("password").clear()
        driver.find_element_by_name("password").send_keys("bpb@123")
        driver.find_element_by_id("tdb1").click()
        driver.find_element_by_link_text("Log Off").click()
        driver.find_element_by_link_text("Continue").click()

    def tearDown(self):
        self.driver.quit()

if __name__ == "__main__":
    unittest.main()
```

Figure 6.1

So in the preceding script, we see the automation test is structured in different sections.

- **setup():** In this, we generally put statements to initialize the browser. Invoke the WebDriver object with the URL we would like to launch.

- **test_login():** In this method, we have written the steps to perform the actual test on the application. Please note that we have not added any assertion action yet. We will see that in the next section.

- **tearDown():** This is the cleanup method. In this we generally put actions to clean up the environment. So here, we have written the statement to close the browser.

Once the structure is complete, we execute the tests by calling the unittest.main() method.

Assertions

Assertions are ways to validate our action. The PyUnit provides us the following set of:

Assert method	Explanation
assertEqual(a, b)	a == b
assertNotEqual(a, b)	a != b
assertTrue(x)	bool(x) is True
assertFalse(x)	bool(x) is False
assertIs(a, b)	a is b

assertIsNot(a, b)	a is not b
assertIsNone(x)	x is None
assertIsNotNone(x)	x is not None
assertIn(a, b)	a in b
assertNotIn(a, b)	a not in b
assertIsInstance(a, b)	isinstance(a, b)
assertNotIsInstance(a, b)	not isinstnace(a, b)
assertRaises(exc, fun, args, *kwds)	fun(*args, **kwds) raises exc
assertRaisesRegexp(exc, r, fun, args, *kwds)	round(a-b, 7) == 0
assertAlmostEqual(a, b)	round(a-b, 7) == 0
assertNotAlmostEqual(a, b)	round(a-b, 7) != 0
assertGreater(a, b)	a > b
assertGreaterEqual(a, b)	a >= b
assertLess(a, b)	a < b
assertLessEqual(a, b)	a <= b
assertRegexpMatches(s, r)	r.search(s)
assertNotRegexpMatches(a, b)	not r.search(s)
assertItemsEqual(a, b)	sorted(a) == sorted(b) Works with unhashable objects
assertDictContains Subset(a, b)	All the key-value pairs in a exist in b

Table 6.1

We will now see a test automation script of login logout where we will use assertion to validate - valid user login, by checking the presence of text My Account Information.

```
def test_login(self):
    driver = self.driver
    driver.get(self.base_url)
    driver.find_element_by_link_text("My Account").click()
    driver.find_element_by_name("email_address").clear()
    driver.find_element_by_name("email_address").send_keys("bpb@bpb.com")
    driver.find_element_by_name("password").clear()
    driver.find_element_by_name("password").send_keys("bpb123")
    driver.find_element_by_id("tdb1").click()
    pgsrc=driver.page_source
    if(pgsrc.index("My Account Information")>-1):
        print("User is Valid")
        driver.find_element_by_link_text("Log Off").click()
        driver.find_element_by_link_text("Continue").click()
        self.assertTrue(True,"User is valid")
    else:
        print("User is Invalid")
        self.assertFalse(False,"User is invalid")
```

Figure 6.2

In the preceding script, we can see usage of `self.assertTrue()` and `self.assertFalse()` statement to mark the test pass or fail depending on the presence of the text **My Account Information**.

Conclusion

So in this chapter we have seenhow can we use the unittest framework to structure our test in `setUp()`, `test_method()` and `teardown()` methods. We have also seen, how we can use assertions to mark our test as pass and fail. You can follow this link, if you want to read more about it- **https://docs.python.org/3/library/unittest.html**.

In the next chapter we will be discuss the concept of waits. We will see how we can synchronize our tests using static and dynamic waits and why is that important.

Questions

1. Explain the structure of a unittest.
2. What does `assertNotEqual()` method do?

CHAPTER 7
Synchronizing Test

In our earlier chapters, we have learnt how do we automate scenarios, identify objects uniquely on a web page and perform actions on them. During automation of scenarios, it is important that we synchronize our tests. So the time it takes for the web application to process, the automation command should match with the speed at which the command is sent by the script to the application.

Structure

- Synchronizing test
- Why synchronization
- Implicit wait
- Explicit wait

Objective

In this chapter we will learnhow we can establish synchronization in our testsso that we ensure our tests are not flaky. Reliable execution is crucial during testing cycles as they help save time, and ensure reliability in test automation exercise. We will learn how we implement that concept in our test scripts.

Synchronization

If we have not implemented synchronization in our tests, then our tests may hover between passing and failing, resulting in flaky tests. To avoid this we should synchronize our tests so that we have a basic reliability in our test behavior. To achieve it we have to apply synchronization in our tests.

There are two kinds of synchronization techniques which we use in test scenarios of Selenium:

- Implicit wait
- Explicit wait

Implicit wait

Implicit wait is a global wait, which applies to every statement in the written test script. An implicit wait, when implemented in the script, tries to find the element on the web page. It will keep polling the web page until the element is found, or till the time is over. If the element is not found within the provided implicit wait, we get an exception `NoSuchElementException`.

In the following program, we will implementimplicit wait:

```python
from selenium import webdriver
import unittest

class Login(unittest.TestCase):
    def setUp(self):
        self.driver =webdriver.Chrome(executable_path= 'D:\Eclipse\BP8\SeleniumwithPython\SeleniumwithPython\drivers\chromedriver.exe')
        self.base_url = "http://practice.bpbonline.com/catalog/index.php"

    def test_login(self):
        driver = self.driver
        driver.get(self.base_url)
        driver.find_element_by_link_text("My Account").click()
        driver.find_element_by_name("email_address").clear()
        driver.find_element_by_name("email_address").send_keys("bpb@bpb.com")
        driver.find_element_by_name("password").clear()
        driver.find_element_by_name("password").send_keys("bpb@123")
        driver.find_element_by_id("tdb1").click()
        driver.find_element_by_link_text("Log Off").click()
        driver.find_element_by_link_text("Continue").click()

    def tearDown(self):
        self.driver.quit()

if __name__ == "__main__":
    unittest.main()
```

Figure 7.1

The command `self.driver.implicity_wait(30)` will apply the wait on every find element command used in the program. So for every statement, it will wait for 30 seconds for the object to appear with the given By locator. It will keep polling the website until it finds the object. If the object is found, the action will be performed on the object. Else after the 30 seconds are over, we will get an exception.

Explicit wait

Explicit wait is basically a local wait which can be implemented either as:

- **Static wait:** It is a forced wait, which is introduced by using `time.sleep(n seconds)` in the code line, whenever we wish to wait in the code for n number of seconds. It is not advisable to use static wait in the code because we generally do not know if the time allocated to wait is less or more. We cannot provide a lot of time to wait in the code, because that will delay our test automation script, and if we provide a very less time, it may result in a flaky test, so such waits are generally unreliable and not advisable.

- **Dynamic wait:** The dynamic wait is implemented in the code with the help of a class called as `WebDriverWait`. This class has a method called as `until()`. In this method we pass an event which may occur and the time units for which we wish to wait for that event to occur. So in this method of `WebDriverWait`, we either wait for an event to occur or it times out. The exception we get in here, in case the event doesn't occur, is `TimedOutException`. But in case the event has occurred, we do not wait for the entire amount of time to finish, we get out of the `until` loop as soon as it's finished.

So, we will have a look at two sets of code in here. In the first example, we will run a positive scenario of login logout using `WebDriverWait`. In the second example we will execute a negative scenario which we will fail forcefully by passing wrong object information in the code. So the method will wait for timeout object to appear:

```
from selenium import webdriver
from selenium.webdriver.common.by import By
from selenium.webdriver.support.ui import WebDriverWait
from selenium.webdriver.support import expected_conditions as EC
import unittest

class Login(unittest.TestCase):
    def setUp(self):
        self.driver = webdriver.Chrome(executable_path=r'D:\tclipse\BPB\SeleniumWithPython\SeleniumWithPython\drivers\chromedriver.exe')
        self.base_url = "http://practice.bpbonline.com/catalog/index.php"

    def test_login(self):
        driver = self.driver
        driver.get(self.base_url)
        driver.find_element_by_link_text("My Account").click()
        driver.find_element_by_name("email_address").clear()
        driver.find_element_by_name("email_address").send_keys("bpb@bpb.com")
        driver.find_element_by_name("password").clear()
        driver.find_element_by_name("password").send_keys("bpb@123")
        driver.find_element_by_id("tdb1").click()
        WebDriverWait(driver, 10).until(
        EC.presence_of_element_located((By.LINK_TEXT, "Log Off")))
        driver.find_element_by_link_text("Log Off").click()
        driver.find_element_by_link_text("Continue").click()

    def tearDown(self):
        self.driver.quit()

if __name__ == "__main__":
    unittest.main()
```

Figure 7.2

The code lines using which we have implemented explicit wait are:

```
WebDriverWait(driver, 10).until(
EC.presence_of_element_located((By.LINK_TEXT, "Log Off")))
```

In the preceding `until()` method, we take an input argument called as `EC.` `presence_of_element_located(By.LINK_TEXT, "Log Off")`, here the `EC` is basically the class called as `expected_conditions` exported from `from selenium.webdriver.support import expected_conditions asEC`. It has a lot of methods available with it which can help trace an event. In the preceding code we have used a method `presence_of_element_located`, so this will basically look for the link with the text `Log Off`, `for 10` seconds. If it finds the link within `10` seconds it will exit the `until` loop and execute the next command, which is clicking on the link, otherwise it will timeout and throw a `TimedOutException`.

Let us try another code example, where we will give a bad locator for `Log Off` link, causing the WebDriver wait method to timeout:

```
WebDriverWait(driver, 10).until(
EC.presence_of_element_located((By.LINK_TEXT, "Log ff")))
driver.find_element_by_link_text("Log Off").click()
```

Figure 7.3

The exception which is thrown is as follows:

```
    raise TimeoutException(message, screen, stacktrace)
selenium.common.exceptions.TimeoutException: Message:
```

Figure 7.4

Conclusion

In this chapter, we have seen how we can use the concept of waits, implicit and explicit wait, in our test automation code and ensure that the scripts are reliable during execution time. By implementing the concept of synchronization we have tried to achieve less flaky tests and introduce predictability in them during execution time. In the next chapter, we will discuss advance type of web elements like table, dropdown, alerts, and frame. We will see how to automate these elements and what all methods are associated with them.

Questions

1. Why synchronization as a concept it important?
2. What is the difference between local wait and global wait?

CHAPTER 8
Concept of Parameterization

Sometimes, we come across situations where we need to execute the same test case, but with every execution we need to use a different data set. Or sometimes, we need to create test data prior to our test suite execution. To resolve all these requirements, we should be familiar with the concept of parameterization.

Structure

- Why do we need parameterization
- What is parameterization
- Creation of test data file
- Parameterizing and login logout scenario

Objective

In this chapter, we will learn how we can use a text file to pass data to our tests and run it as many times as rows are available in our file. With this, we will understand the concept of parameterization.

Test data file

Test cases generally need test data for execution. When we write scripts to automate the test, it could be possible that we have hard coded the test data within the test scripts. The drawback of this approach is if our test data needs to be changed for a test execution cycle, we will need to make changes at the test script level, thus making it prone to errors. So a good test script is when test data is kept outside the code.

To achieve the same, we need to parameterize our tests. In this we replace the hard code values in the test with variables. At the time of execution, these variables are replaced by valueswhich are picked from external data sources. These data sources could be text files, excel sheets, databases, JSON, XML, and others.

Parameterization and login logout scenario

Selenium doesn't provide any provision to parameterize the tests. We write the code to parameterize the test using the programming language. In this chapter we will see how we can parameterize our test using a CSV file, and an excel file. The scenario we are going to pick is the login logout scenario, and we will parameterize it using two datasets--first dataset will be for valid user and password combination. And the second dataset will be for a bad username and password combination.

The data to be picked for the test is available in a file called `login.csv`, which is kept in the dataset folder in the project. Refer to following screenshot:

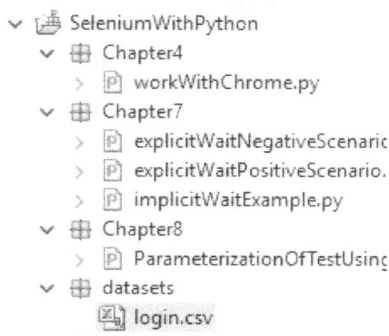

Figure 8.1

The dataset file login .csv has the following data:

```
bpb@bpb.com,bpb@123
abc@demo.com,demo123
```

Figure 8.2

In a CSV file, the data is separated by a *comma*. The test script provided below, reads the data using Python file handling commands and splits it based on a comma. It then passes these values for username and password in the script. The following test iterates twice, which is equal to the number of rows in this file:

```
from selenium import webdriver
import unittest

class Login(unittest.TestCase):
    def setUp(self):
        self.driver = webdriver.Chrome(executable_path="D:\Eclipse\BPB\SeleniumWithPython\SeleniumWithPython\drivers\chromedriver.exe")
        self.driver.implicitly_wait(30)
        self.base_url = "http://practice.bpbonline.com/catalog/index.php"

    def test_login(self):
        driver = self.driver
        driver.get(self.base_url)
        file = open("D:\Eclipse\BPB\SeleniumWithPython\SeleniumWithPython\datasets\login.csv", "r")
        for line in file:
            driver.find_element_by_link_text("My Account").click()
            data=line.split(",")
            print(data)
            driver.find_element_by_name("email_address").send_keys(data[0])
            driver.find_element_by_name("password").send_keys(data[1].strip())
            driver.find_element_by_id("tdb1").click()
            if(driver.page_source.find("My Account Information")!=-1):
                driver.find_element_by_link_text("Log Off").click()
                driver.find_element_by_link_text("Continue").click()
                print("Valid user credential")
            else:
                print("Bad user credential")
        file.close()

    def tearDown(self):
        self.driver.quit()

if __name__ == "__main__":
    unittest.main()
```

Figure 8.3

In the preceding program, we have written the scenario of login logout, but it is wrapped around a while loop. This while loop is basically reading file contents, until the end of file is reached. So the entire script will execute as many times as the number of rows in the file.

As we execute the test, we will see that it passes for the first data set picked from the file, as it is a combination of valid username and password. But for the second dataset the test reports a failure. The preceding test will execute for as many rows as available in our login.csv dataset file.

Conclusion

In this chapter we have learned how to use test data for our tests, and the importance of keeping test data separate from the actual tests. We also saw how we can read data from a CSV file or a text-based file, and pass them to our test code.

In our next chapter we will learn how to handle different types of web elements.

Questions

1. Why do we need parameterization at test case level?
2. Can automation be used to create test data required to be consumed by the test suite during automation?

CHAPTER 9

Working with Different WebElements

An HTML page is made up of various HTML elements. When we automate a web page using Selenium, we first have to identify the HTML element uniquely on the web page and then perform an action on it. An HTML page can have HTML elements like a form, frame, table, dropdown, link, image, alerts, div, spans, and many more. In this chapter we will learn how to automate these elements through Selenium.

Structure
- Working with form elements
- Working with HTML table
- Working with dropdown list

Objective

An HTML page is made up of different HTML elements, for example, we see a form element, which contains a lot of input elements. The input elements could be a textbox, radio button, or checkbox. We can then have a table element, a dropdown element. In this chapter we will see how we can automate these HTML elements.

Working with form elements

An HTML form generally contains text boxes, buttons, links, images, radio buttons, and checkboxes type of elements. The HTML of the input elements in the form is represented as follows:

```
<input type= "text/checkbox/radio/password property=value..
/>
```

The following table shows the different actions we generally perform on these elements using Selenium:

WebElement	Selenium action	Description
Text box	Clear	Clears the content of the textbox.
Text box	send_keys	Types content sent in the method in the textbox.
Checkbox	Click	To select a given checkbox.
Radio button	Click	To select a given radio button.
Anchor	Click	To click on the link element.
Button	Click	To click on the button in the form.
Button	Submit	If the button provided is a submit button, then we can perform the submit action on it.
Radio button		To verify if the radio button is selected.
HTML element		This method will work for any HTML element, and it checks if the element is displayed on the page or not.
HTML element	IsEnabled	This method will work for any HTML element, and it checks if the element is enabled on the page or not.

Table 9.1

An example of working on the form elements described above can be seen on the registration page of the application: **http://practice. bpbonline.com/catalog/create_account.php**

On this page, we can see checkbox, radio button, textboxes, button, links on which we can work. The following program displays the process of user registration by performing actions on the different web elements on this page:

```python
def test_login(self):
    browser=self.driver
    browser.get(self.base_url)
    browser.find_element_by_link_text("My Account").click()
    browser.find_element_by_link_text("Continue").click()
    browser.find_element_by_name("gender").click()
    browser.find_element_by_name("firstname").send_keys("BPB")
    browser.find_element_by_name("lastname").send_keys("BPB")
    browser.find_element_by_id("dob").send_keys("01/01/1987")
    #change email id with each iteration
    browser.find_element_by_name("email_address").send_keys("bpb1@bpb.com")
    browser.find_element_by_name("company").send_keys("5Elements Learning")
    browser.find_element_by_name("street_address").send_keys("First Address")
    browser.find_element_by_name("suburb").send_keys("Second Address")
    browser.find_element_by_name("postcode").send_keys("110001")
    browser.find_element_by_name("city").send_keys("New Delhi")
    browser.find_element_by_name("state").send_keys("Delhi")
    sel=Select(browser.find_element_by_name("country"))
    sel.select_by_visible_text("India")
    browser.find_element_by_name("country")
    browser.find_element_by_name("telephone").send_keys("1234567890")
    browser.find_element_by_name("fax").send_keys("0123456789")
    browser.find_element_by_name("newsletter").click()
    browser.find_element_by_name("password").send_keys("123456")
    browser.find_element_by_name("confirmation").send_keys("123456")
    browser.find_element_by_xpath("//span[contains(text(), 'Continue')]").click()
    browser.find_element_by_xpath("//span[contains(text(), 'Continue')]").click()
    browser.find_element_by_link_text("Log Off").click()
    browser.find_element_by_link_text("Continue").click()
```

Figure 9.1

So in the preceding code, we are registering a new user in the applicationby handling actions on all the mandatory fields. So wherever there are textboxes, we have ensured they are cleared first, and then we type the text on them. For links, buttons, and radio buttons, we have used the click method for selecting them.

Working with HTML tables

The HTML tables are container elements, which mean they contain other HTML elements inside them. A general representation of HTML table is as follows:

```
<table>
<tbody>
<tr>
<td> text/HTML element</td>
<td> … </td>
</tr>
<tr>…</tr>
</tbody>
</table>
```

So we have the first node as table, which contains tbody, which contains table row[tr]. The tr node contains table data[td] which represents the table cell. The table cell can contain text or any HTML element within it. In our application, the home page displays the products listed in a web table:

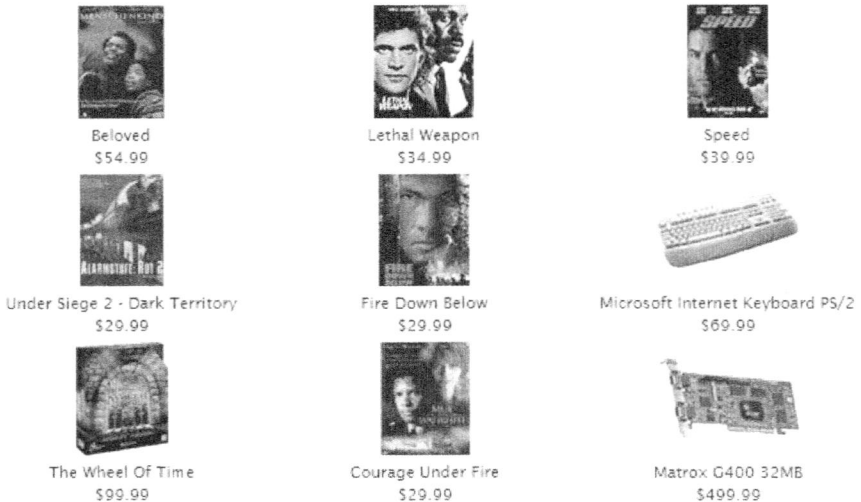

Beloved
$54.99

Lethal Weapon
$34.99

Speed
$39.99

Under Siege 2 - Dark Territory
$29.99

Fire Down Below
$29.99

Microsoft Internet Keyboard PS/2
$69.99

The Wheel Of Time
$99.99

Courage Under Fire
$29.99

Matrox G400 32MB
$499.99

Figure 9.2

Let us look at the backend HTML available:

```
▼<table border="0" width="100%" cellspacing="0" cellpadding="2">
  ▼<tbody>
    ▼<tr>
      ▼<td width="33%" align="center" valign="top">
        ▶<a href="http://practice.bpbonline.com/catalog/product_info.php?
          products_id=20">...</a>
          <br>
          <a href="http://practice.bpbonline.com/catalog/product_info.php?
          products_id=20">Beloved</a>
          <br>
          "$54.99"
        </td>
      ▶<td width="33%" align="center" valign="top">...</td>
      ▶<td width="33%" align="center" valign="top">...</td>
    </tr>
  ▶<tr>...</tr>
  ▶<tr>...</tr>
```

Figure 9.3

As we see in the preceding HTML snippet, the table has three `tr` tags, and each `tr` tag has three `td` tags. Each `td` tag has two anchor tags and a text, which we see on the page. One of the scenarios we pick for HTML web table automation is to find the rows and columns available in the table at run time. Here, we will be doing that, and printing the content available in every table cell as we iterate the table row by row and cell by cell.

```python
from selenium import webdriver
import unittest

class TableExample(unittest.TestCase):
    def setUp(self):
        self.driver = webdriver.Chrome(executable_path=r'D:\Eclipse\BPB\SeleniumWithPython\SeleniumWithPython\drivers\chromedriver.exe')
        self.driver.implicitly_wait(30)
        self.base_url = "http://practice.bpbonline.com/catalog/index.php"
    def test_table(self):
        driver = self.driver
        driver.get(self.base_url)
        prodTable=driver.find_element_by_tag_name("table")

        rows=prodTable.find_elements_by_xpath(".//*/tbody/tr")
        i=1
        for r in rows:
            cols=r.find_elements_by_xpath("td")

            j=1
            for cd in cols:
                print("row ",i, "col ", j, " ", cd.text)
                j=j+1
            i=i+1

    def tearDown(self):
        self.driver.quit()

if __name__ == "__main__":
    unittest.main()
```

Figure 9.4

So in the preceding code, we first fetch the table object, then in that table object we fetch all the table rows. Then we iterate each table row, and fetch all table columns from each row. Then we iterate each table column, and fetch the text associated with each table cell, and print that information on the screen.

As we run the test, the output is as follows:

```
row:  1 col:  1 - Fire Down Below
$29.99
row:  1 col:  2 - Microsoft Internet Keyboard PS/2
$69.99
row:  1 col:  3 - The Wheel Of Time
$99.99
row:  2 col:  1 - Courage Under Fire
$29.99
row:  2 col:  2 - Matrox G400 32MB
$499.99
row:  2 col:  3 - SWAT 3: Close Quarters Battle
$79.99
row:  3 col:  1 - You've Got Mail
$34.99
row:  3 col:  2 - A Bug's Life
$35.99
row:  3 col:  3 - Hewlett Packard LaserJet 1100Xi
$499.99
```

Figure 9.5

Working with dropdown list

The dropdown list in HTML is known as the `<select>` element. It is also a container element. It contains `<option>` elements. The option element displays the different choices of the dropdown which can be selected from it. The HTML code of dropdown looks as follows:

```
<select>

<option value = data> Visible text </option>

..

</select>
```

In our application, dropdown are available at various pages. The dropdown element which we will see in example is the country dropdown which we see on the registration page of the application:

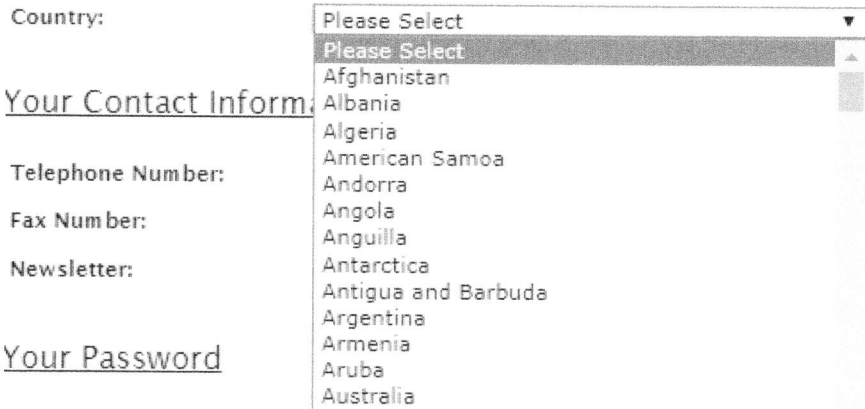

Country: Please Select   ▼
                            Please Select   ▲
                            Afghanistan
Your Contact Inform: Albania
                            Algeria
                            American Samoa
Telephone Number: Andorra
                            Angola
Fax Number: Anguilla
                            Antarctica
Newsletter: Antigua and Barbuda
                            Argentina
                            Armenia
Your Password   Aruba
                            Australia

Figure 9.6

If we look at the backend HTML of this dropdown, we will see the following:

```
▼<select name="country">
    <option value selected="selected">Please Select</option>
    <option value="1">Afghanistan</option>
    <option value="2">Albania</option>
    <option value="3">Algeria</option>
    <option value="4">American Samoa</option>
    <option value="5">Andorra</option>
    <option value="6">Angola</option>
    <option value="7">Anguilla</option>
    <option value="8">Antarctica</option>
    <option value="9">Antigua and Barbuda</option>
    <option value="10">Argentina</option>
    <option value="11">Armenia</option>
    <option value="12">Aruba</option>
```

Figure 9.7

The number of options in the list will be the same as we see on the screen.

To work with a dropdown element, Selenium provides a separate class called `Select`. More details on this class can be found on this link:

**https://seleniumhq.github.io/selenium/docs/api/py/
webdriver_support/selenium.webdriver.support.select.
HTML?highlight=select# selenium.webdriver.support.select**

The `Select` class allows us to select an element from the list using the following three methods:

- `select_by_value`: In this method, we select an option by passing the data associated with the value attribute. For example in the previous list, if we say `select_by_value("5")`, Andorra as a country will get selected.

- `select_by_visible_text`: In this method, we select an option by passing the data which we see on the screen. For example, if we want to select the country `Angola`, we can say `select_by_visible_text("Angola")`.

- `select_by_index`: In this method, we select an option from the list, by passing an index value. The index value associated with the options in the list ranges from 0 to the total number of options `-1`. So if we say `select_by_index(2)`, `Albania` will get selected.

Similar to the preceding set of methods, we have select by value, visible text, and index. In the following program:

```python
def test_dropdown(self):
    browser=self.driver
    browser.get(self.base_url)
    browser.maximize_window()
    browser.find_element_by_link_text("My Account").click()
    browser.find_element_by_link_text("Continue").click()
    sel=Select(browser.find_element_by_name("country"))
    #select by visible text
    sel.select_by_visible_text("India")
    print(sel.first_selected_option.text)
    time.sleep(1)
    #select by index
    sel.select_by_index(1)
    print(sel.first_selected_option.text)
    time.sleep(1)
    #select by value
    sel.select_by_value("5")
    print(sel.first_selected_option.text)
    time.sleep(1)

    #find an option in the list
    for country in sel.options:
        if(country.text == "India"):
            print("country found")
```

Figure 9.8

In the preceding program, we try different methods to select options from the dropdown element. We use a method called first_ selected_option, which returns the option that was selected first and foremost in the list.

Conclusion

So in this chapter we have seen how to handle different types of form elements, web table elements, and the dropdown element. We saw the different methods that are available with these entities. We also saw the different actions which can be performed on the HTML elements during test automation runs. In the next chapter we will discuss the switch To method, and see how we can handle frames, alerts with it. We will also see the action class which allows us to handle various keyboard, mouse actions, and also automate composite actions.

Questions

1. Which HTML tag is used for dropdown element?
2. Can web element be used to handle dropdown element?
3. Name a few methods of the Select class in Selenium.

CHAPTER 10

Frames, Alerts, and Action Class

In this chapter, we will learn about the concept of switchTo() command associated with the driver object. Many a times we come across applications which have a frame in them, if we have to handle the objects in a frame we need to first switch to the frame, and only then can we work on the objects of the page in the frame. Another usage of switch is seen in handling alerts, JavaScript pop windows, which come up to ask for *yes* or *no / ok* and *cancel* decisions, to proceed. And lastly, we are going to talk about the action class, which allows us to automate various mouse and keyboard movements. It also allows us to automate composite action class.

Structure

- Working with frame
- Working with alerts
- Action class

Objective

The WebDriver element has a method called switchTo(). This method allows switching the focus to a frame, an alert, or a new window. In this chapter we will see its usage. Another entity we will see is the `Action` class. This is used to automate keyboard and mouse actions. Sometimes, we may come across composite actions, and in those situations, actions class is helpful.

Working with frame

A frame HTML element allows us to break an HTML window into multiple sections, where each section can contain its own HTML page. A frame tag is represented inside a frameset tag and looks like the following:

```
<frameset>

<frame name="topframe" src="topframe.htm">

<frame name="botframe" src="botframe.htm">

</frameset>
```

If we have to work with the HTML element which is available in the web page that lies inside a frame, we need to switch to the frame first and only then we can interact with the HTML elements of the page inside the frame. To perform this task we need to use the `switch_to()` command, using some attribute identify the frame which contains the element. Let us take the following example of a page which contains nested frames: **http://the-internet.herokuapp.com/nested_frames.**

If we look at the backend HTML of the page, we will find that the page contains a top frame, and a bottom frame. The top frame further contains three frames: left, middle and right. The following screenshot shows the frames HTML:

```
▼<frameset frameborder="1" rows="50%,50%">
  ▼<frame src="/frame_top" scrolling="no" name="frame-top">
    ▼#document
      ▼<html>
          <script src="chrome-extension://cdmedbnojkdahhdbjnemegblhbaalkbc/page/prompt.js">
          </script>
          <script src="chrome-extension://cdmedbnojkdahhdbjnemegblhbaalkbc/page/runScript.js">
          </script>
        ►<head>...</head>
        ▼<frameset frameborder="1" name="frameset-middle" cols="33%,33%,33%">
          ►<frame src="/frame_left" scrolling="no" name="frame-left">...</frame>
          ►<frame src="/frame_middle" scrolling="no" name="frame-middle">...</frame> == $0
          ►<frame src="/frame_right" scrolling="no" name="frame-right">...</frame>
          </frameset>
        </html>
      </frame>
  ►<frame src="/frame_bottom" scrolling="no" name="frame-bottom">...</frame>
```

Figure 10.1

Now, let us suppose that in the preceding example we need to fetch the text associated with the page inside the middle frame, so how will we do that? To achieve this we will first need to switch to the top frame, and then from it, switch to the middle frame. Once we have switched to the middle frame we can fetch the text associated with it. The following program shows the working of the same.

```
from selenium import webdriver
import unittest

class FrameExample(unittest.TestCase):
    def setUp(self):
        self.driver = webdriver.Chrome(executable_path="c:\\ecl\paseworkspace\seleniumwithPython\seleniumwithPython\drivers\chromed-ver.exe")
        self.driver.implicitly_wait(30)
        self.base_url = "https://the-internet.herokuapp.com/nested_frames"

    def test_frame(self):
        driver = self.driver
        driver.get(self.base_url)
        driver.switch_to_frame(driver.find_element_by_name("frame-top"))
        driver.switch_to_frame(driver.find_element_by_name("frame-middle"))
        print(driver.page_source)

    def tearDown(self):
        self.driver.quit()

if __name__ == "__main__":
    unittest.main()
```

Figure 10.2

In the preceding program, we switch our focus to the first frame which is recognized by the name property `frame-top`, and then we switch our focus to another frame inside it which is recognized by the name property `frame-middle`. Once we have switched focus to the inner frame, we print the page source of it.

The output which we get when we run the program is as follows:

```
<html xmlns="http://www.w3.org/1999/xhtml"><head>
    </head>
    <body>
        <div id="content">MIDDLE</div>


</body></html>
```

Figure 10.3

Working with alerts

Alerts are JavaScript popup windows which prompt the user for an action or decision based on which an event is performed, or it displays some information to the user. For example, in our web application **http://practice.bpbonline.com/catalog/index.php,** when we try to register the user, and while filling in the registration form, if we forget to fill in some mandatory field and we try to proceed with the process, we will see an alert prompting us to correct our entries.

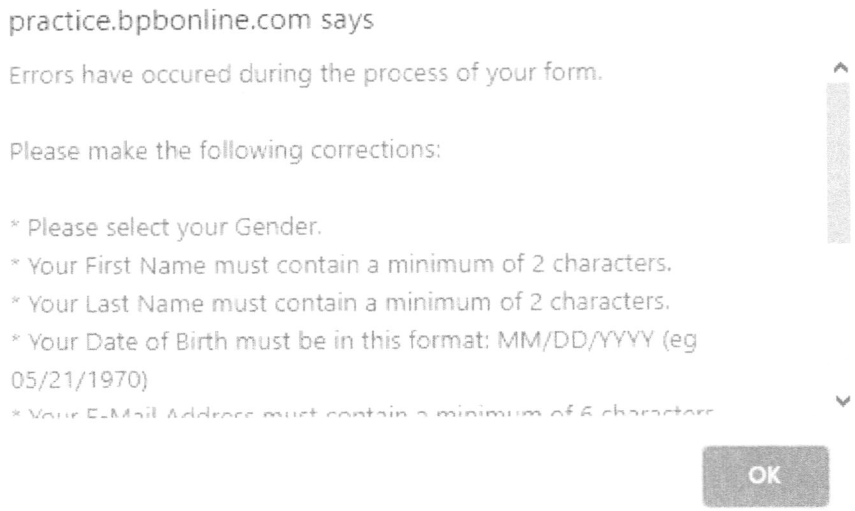

practice.bpbonline.com says

Errors have occured during the process of your form.

Please make the following corrections:

* Please select your Gender.
* Your First Name must contain a minimum of 2 characters.
* Your Last Name must contain a minimum of 2 characters.
* Your Date of Birth must be in this format: MM/DD/YYYY (eg 05/21/1970)
* Your F-Mail Address must contain a minimum of 6 characters

OK

Figure 10.4

Now to handle the preceding alert we have to click on the **OK** button. To perform the action we have a class available in Selenium called the `Alert` class. The details of it are available here: **https://seleniumhq. github.io/selenium/docs/api/py/webdriver/selenium.webdriver. common.alert.html.** This `Alert` class has four methods:

- `accept()`: It accepts the alert by clicking on the **OK** button.
- `dismiss()`: It cancels the alert by clicking on the cancel button.
- `Send_keys`: It sends keys to the alert.
- `Text`: It fetches the text associated with the alert.

The scenario from our application which we try to automateis the user registration process. Here, we will first pass a bad combination of password and confirm password. This will cause the alert to popup:

practice.bpbonline.com says

Errors have occured during the process of your form.

Please make the following corrections:

* The Password Confirmation must match your Password.

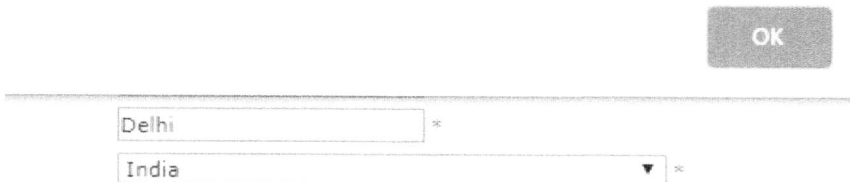

OK

Delhi   *

India   ▼ ×

Figure 10.5

So, we use the `Alert` class here, and its method accepts to handle it, as can be seen in the following code snippet:

```
#bad password and confirm password
browser.find_element_by_name("password").send_keys("123456")
browser.find_element_by_name("confirmation").send_keys("1234")
browser.find_element_by_xpath("//span[@class='ui-button-text'][contains(text(), 'Continue')]").click()
time.sleep(3)
alert=browser.switch_to_alert()
print(alert.text)
alert.accept() #works on OK button
time.sleep(3)
#provide correct pad and confirm pwd
browser.find_element_by_name("password").clear()
browser.find_element_by_name("password").send_keys("123456")
browser.find_element_by_name("confirmation").clear()
```

Figure 10.6

The complete code of the preceding snippet is available in the code base.

Action class

Selenium provides us with an action class, in its Python implementation it is known as **action chains**. This class helps us to handle low level keyboard and mouse actions as well as complex actions like drag and drop, mouse hover, and more. Using the `Action` class, you can either call one action at a time, or you can queue up the actions one after another and then use a method called as `perform()` to call them in order. We will take an example here for a website to perform drag and drop action. This example will also showcase usage of frame.

So the website we will be using hereis: **http://jqueryui.com/droppable/**

There are two objects, where the left one has to be dropped on right. Refer to the following diagram:

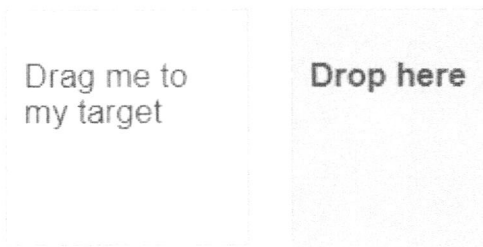

Drag me to my target   **Drop here**

Figure 10.7

As we inspect the element, we will find that these elements are inside the `iframe tag`. Let us have a look:

```
▼<iframe src="/resources/demos/droppable/default.html" class="demo-frame">
  ▼#document
      <!doctype html>
    ▼<html lang="en">
      ▶<head>…</head>
      ▼<body>
        ▶<div id="draggable" class="ui-widget-content ui-draggable ui-draggable-
        handle" style="position: relative;">…</div>
        ▶<div id="droppable" class="ui-widget-header ui-droppable">…</div>
      </body>
    </html>
</iframe>
```

Figure 10.8

We want to drag the left object and drop it on the right object. The following code shows how we can do that:

```
driver = self.driver
driver.get(self.base_url)
actions = ActionChains(driver)
driver.switch_to_frame(driver.find_element_by_class_name("demo-frame"))
draggable=driver.find_element_by_id("draggable");
droppable=driver.find_element_by_id("droppable");
actions.drag_and_drop(draggable, droppable).perform();
time.sleep(3)
```

Figure 10.9

In the preceding program, we first switch to the `iframe` which contains the draggable and droppable objects. We then recognize the objects using their ID properties. Once the objects are created, we use the method available with the `Action` class, `drag_and_drop()`, which performs the required action and solves the scenario.

So to use the `ActionChains` class, we have to import it as well, so the following would be our import modules:

`from selenium.webdriver.common.action_chains import ActionChains`

Conclusion

In this chapter, we saw how we will handle the frame HTML element, by using the `switchTo` command. Also, if we come across the JavaScript popups, how do we handle them using the alert interface available in Selenium. If we come across scenarios in application which require composite actions like click and hold, drag and drop, double click, context click, we have with us `Action` class, which we can use to handle mouse actions, keyboard actions, and composite actions as well.

In our next chapter we will learn about the concept of **Page Object Model (POM)**, where we will learn how we handle object information. The management of object information is important and is required for our test automation scripts.

Questions

1. To which all entities will `switchTo()` work for?
2. What does the function `contextClick()` do in `Action` class?
3. What is the function of the `perform()` method?

CHAPTER 11
Page Object Model

Selenium is an open source test automation tool. Like other commercial tools in the market it doesn't come up with any inbuilt feature to manage object information which we use in creating test scripts. So we need to take help of design patterns like POM to manage these artifacts. In this chapter we will understand how to create them and what benefits they bring to the table.

Structure

- Page Object Model (POM)
- Implementing the POM
- Example of login logout scenario

Objective

This chapter will help us understand the concept of a design pattern called as **Page Object Model (POM),** and how to implement it to make our scripts more robust.

Page Object Model (POM)

Page Object Model (POM) is a design pattern which helps us to separate the object information from the business logic of a page from the application. The idea behind this is, if the object information changes from one build release to another, the business logic is not impacted at the code level, and we only make changes at the object information level. To achieve this we need to implement POM design pattern at our code level.

Creating Selenium test cases can result in an un-maintainable project. One of the reasons is that too much of duplicated code is used. Duplicated code could be caused by duplicated functionality and this will result in duplicated usage of locator information to identify the objects on a page. The disadvantage of duplicated code is that the project is less maintainable. If some locator will change, you have to walk through the whole test code to adjust locators where necessary.

Implementing the POM

By using the POM we can make non-brittle test code and reduce or eliminate duplicate test code. Besides, it improves the readability and allows us to create interactive documentation. Last but not least, we can create tests with less keystrokes.

The concept of POM says that when we look at a page, we should see as if it has got two components:

- Objects
- Business logic

So the page has a business logic, and to achieve that business objective there are objects available on the page. We need to segregate these two entities. The reason for this is, over a period of time as an application undergoes changes the object information can get changed more frequently, making the maintenance of the code a humongous effort. Let us take an example of the **My Account Page** here from our application: **http://practice.bpbonline.com/catalog/login.php**

The business logic of the page says:

- If there exists a new user, allow them to create a new account.
- If there is a registered user with valid credentials allow them to login.

- If there is a registered user, but who has forgotten credentials, allow them to fetch the password.
- Not allow a user with invalid credentials to login.

To achieve these business functions, the page is designed with the following objects:

- Username textbox
- Password textbox
- Sign in button
- Continue button

Please find the following screenshot explaining the preceding bullet points:

Returning Customer   New Customer

I am a returning customer.   I am a new customer.

E-Mail Address: [   ]   By creating an account at BPBOnline you will be able to
                                              shop faster, be up to date on an orders status, and keep
Password: [   ]   track of the orders you have previously made.

Password forgotten? Click here.   ▶ Continue

                          🔑 Sign In

Figure 11.1

By keeping object information separate from business logic, we are able to manage and achieve modularity and robustness at the code level. As we find during build release cycles, the object information may change over a period of time, so only the files where object information is stored needs to be changed, whereas the test logic which is consuming these objects will not get affected by it.

In this chapter, we will see how we will implement POM for the login logout scenario of our application.

First we will create the file to capture the object information:

```
from selenium.webdriver.common.by import By

# for maintainability we can seperate web objects by page name

class MainPageLocators(object):
    MYACCOUNT      = (By.LINK_TEXT, 'My Account')


class LoginPageLocators(object):
    EMAIL       = (By.NAME, 'email_address')
    PASSWORD    = (By.NAME, 'password')
    SIGNIN      = (By.ID, 'tdb1')



class LogoutPageLocators(object):
    LOGOFF      = (By.LINK_TEXT, 'Log Off')
    CONTINUE    = (By.LINK_TEXT, 'Continue')
```

Figure 11.2

So, if the object information in any of the upcoming builds changes, we can come to this file, and change the information associated with that object.

In another file, called as `pages.py` we call the action associated with each object:

```
class MainPage(Page):
    def click_myaccount(self):
        self.find_element(*MainPageLocators.MYACCOUNT).click()
        return self.driver

class LoginPage(Page):
    def enter_email(self, email):
        self.find_element(*LoginPageLocators.EMAIL).send_keys(email)

    def enter_password(self,pwd):
        self.find_element(*LoginPageLocators.PASSWORD).send_keys(pwd)

    def click_login_button(self):
        self.find_element(*LoginPageLocators.SIGNIN).click()

    def login(self, email,pwd):
        self.enter_email(email)
        self.enter_password(pwd)
        self.click_login_button()
        return self.driver


class LogoutPage(Page):
    def click_logoff(self):
        self.find_element(*LogoutPageLocators.LOGOFF).click()

    def click_continue(self):
        self.find_element(*LogoutPageLocators.CONTINUE).click()

    def logout(self):
        self.click_logoff()
        self.click_continue()
```

Figure 11.3

Now, we will create the test scenarios:

```
def test_sign_in_with_valid_user(self):
    mainPage = MainPage(self.driver)
    mainPage.click_myaccount()
    loginPage=LoginPage(self.driver)
    loginPage.login("bpb@bpb.com","bpb@123")
    logoutPage=LogoutPage(self.driver)
    logoutPage.logout()
```

Figure 11.4

As we can see, our actual test scenario looks clean, easy to read. Since object information is now hidden in the other files, the test can concentrate on actual test logic.

Conclusion

In this chapter, we learnt the importance and need for POM to manage and maintain object information in the form of page objects. This is necessary as Selenium by default doesn't come with any feature like object repository to manage and maintain object information. POM helps us create a modular and robust code.

In our next chapter, we will discuss the concept of Selenium Grid, which as a component, allows us to execute scenarios in parallel.

Questions

1. What do you understand by **Page Object Model (POM)**?
2. Create a POM for the buy product scenario

CHAPTER 12
Selenium -Grid

Parallel execution of tests is made possible in Seleniumthrough its Grid component. We come across scenarios like executing tests for cross browser verification, or executing a huge test suite by splitting it into smaller suites in parallel to save time. For all these, Grid component is useful and effective as it allows parallel test execution.

Structure

- Selenium-Grid
- Creating hub
- Creating nodes
- Executing tests in parallel

Objective

In this chapter, we learn how to setup Selenium-Grid in our local system. We understand what is a hub and a node, and how we set them up. In this chapter, we will set up a hub that will act as a central server and receive requests. We will have a Chrome node, and a

Firefox node to complete the Grid for execution.

Selenium-Grid

An important component of Selenium is the Selenium-Grid. It allows us to run our tests in parallel,which helps in saving time and cost. To set up the Selenium-Grid, we need to first download the Selenium standalone server from: **https://www.seleniumhq.org/download/**

After we have downloaded the server JAR file, we will store it in a folder. This JAR file can now be invoked in two different modes to setup the Grid:

- The hub
- The node

A hub is the central server which receives the request to execute the test. It will send the testto the node in the Grid which matches with the description in the test. While anode is a machine and browser combination where actual execution of the test takes place.

Let us see a Grid setup, with the help of the following diagram:

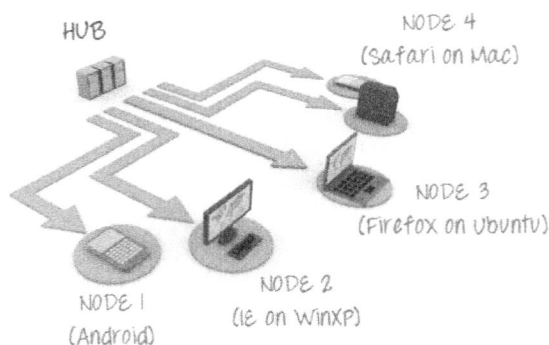

Figure 12.1: Grid setup

In the above diagram, we can see that the hub will receive the test execution request, which will get passed on to the matching node for actual execution. As the test is executed at the node, the result is passed back to the hub. The information, about the browser, and the operating system on which the test is to be executed, is present in the test script which the hub receives. Then the test commands are sent to the matched node for the actual execution.

We will nowsetup a Grid with one hub and two nodes--one for Chrome and another for Firefox. Let us see the commands for it.

Setting up the hub

To setup the hub, we need to open the Command Prompt window and go to the folder where our standalone JAR file is present. There we need to type the following command:

```
D:\WORK\JarFiles>java -jar selenium-server-standalone-3.141.59.jar -role hub
```

Figure 12.2

In the above command, we are executing the standalone JAR file using the `role` flag that uses the value `hub`. So it will execute the server in the hub mode. By default, it will start the hub on the port 4444.

If we want to change the port, we can use the `-port` flag and provide a value to it. For example:

```
D:\WORK\JarFiles>java -jar selenium-server-standalone-3.141.59.jar -role hub -port 6666
```

Figure 12.3

If you are working with a different Selenium standalone server version, the version number will change for you in here.

Once the hub has started, you can verify it using the following steps:

1. Open a browser.
2. Type this URL:

   `http://localhost:4444/grid/console`

3. If all is working fine, you should be able to see the following:

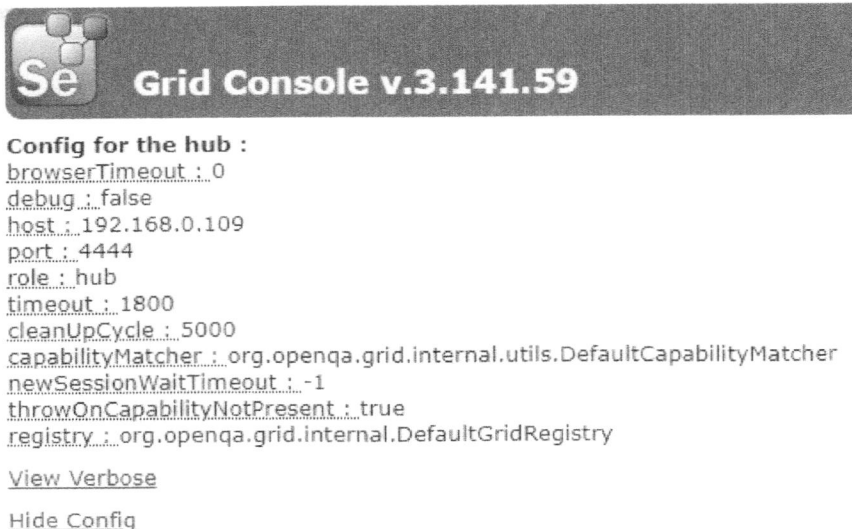

Grid Console v.3.141.59

Config for the hub :
browserTimeout : 0
debug : false
host : 192.168.0.109
port : 4444
role : hub
timeout : 1800
cleanUpCycle : 5000
capabilityMatcher : org.openqa.grid.internal.utils.DefaultCapabilityMatcher
newSessionWaitTimeout : -1
throwOnCapabilityNotPresent : true
registry : org.openqa.grid.internal.DefaultGridRegistry

View Verbose

Hide Config

Figure 12.4

At the Command Prompt, we will see the following:

```
D:\WORK\JarFiles>java -jar selenium-server-standalone-3.141.59.jar -role hub
17:17:17.540 INFO [GridLauncherV3.parse] - Selenium server version: 3.141.59, revision: e82
be7d358
17:17:17.665 INFO [GridLauncherV3.lambda$buildLaunchers$5] - Launching Selenium Grid hub on
 port 4444
2019-05-27 17:17:18.139:INFO::main: Logging initialized @1218ms to org.seleniumhq.jetty9.ut
il.log.StdErrLog
17:17:18.576 INFO [Hub.start] - Selenium Grid hub is up and running
17:17:18.576 INFO [Hub.start] - Nodes should register to http://192.168.0.109:4444/grid/reg
ister/
17:17:18.576 INFO [Hub.start] - Clients should connect to http://192.168.0.109:4444/wd/hub
```

Figure 12.5

Setting a Chrome node on Windows machine

To set a Chrome node on a Windows machine, we will have to download the Selenium standalone server on that machine, and execute it in the node mode. To do this, we will have execute this command:

```
D:\WORK\JarFiles>java -Dwebdriver.chrome.driver="D:\WORK\JarFiles\resource\chromedriver.exe" -jar selenium-server-standa
lone-3.141.59.jar -role node -hub http://localhost:4444/grid/register -browser "browserName=chrome" -port 5556
```

Figure 12.6

In theis command, we are providing a path to the Chrome driver as per the location in our system, that is, `Dwebdriver.chrome.driver="D:\WORK\JarFiles\resource\chromedriver.exe"`. Then we set the `role` flag to be the `node`. Then we provide the `hub` flag, where we point the hub location: `http://localhost:4444/grid/register`. We set the browser flag to `chrome` and port flag to `5556`.

At the script level, we will be making some changes in the setup method, which is as follows:

```python
def setUp(self):
    self.driver = webdriver.Remote(
        command_executor="http://localhost:4444/wd/hub",
        desired_capabilities={
            "browserName": "chrome",
        })

    self.base_url = "http://practice.bpbonline.com/catalog/index.php"
```

Figure 12.7

Here, we create an instance of the remote WebDriver, pass the details of the hub and in desired capabilities variable, we pass information for the browser, on which we want to execute our test, in this case, Chrome. We will discuss more about desired capabilities a little later in the chapter. So when we execute the script, the commands are sent to the hub. It fetches the information to find the node on which the actual test is to be executed and send the commands to it. In this case it will send the commands to a node which is registered with a Chrome browser.

Please take a look at the following screenshot where we have entered all the details:

Largest Publisher Of Computer Books

Welcome, Please Sign In

Returning Customer

I am a returning customer.

E-Mail Address: bpb@bpb.com

Password: ●●●●●●

Password forgotten? Click here.

🔑 Sign In

New Customer

I am a new customer.

By creating an account at BPBOnline you will be able to shop faster, be up to date on an orders status, and keep track of the orders you have previously made.

› Continue

Figure 12.8

Setting a Firefox node on Windows machine

To set a Firefox node on a Windows machine, we will have to download the Selenium standalone server on that machine, and execute it in the node mode. To do this we will have execute this command:

```
D:\WORK\JarFiles>java -Dwebdriver.gecko.driver="D:\WORK\JarFiles\resource\geckodriver.exe" -jar selenium-server-standalo
ne-3.141.59.jar -role node -hub http://localhost:4444/grid/register -browser "browserName=firefox" -port 5557
```

Figure 12.9

In this command,we are providing the path to the gecko driver as per the location in our system: `Dwebdriver.gecko.driver="D:\WORK\JarFiles\resource\geckodriver.exe"`. Then we set the `role` flag to be `node`. Then we provide the hub flag, where we point the hub location: `http://localhost:4444/grid/register`. We set the browser flag to `firefox` and port flag to `5557`.

At the script level, we will be making some changes in the setup method:

```python
def setUp(self):
    self.driver  = webdriver.Remote(
        command_executor="http://localhost:4444/wd/hub",
        desired_capabilities={
            "browserName": "firefox",
        })

    self.base_url = "http://practice.bpbonline.com/catalog/index.php"
```

Figure 12.10

Here, we create an instance of the remote WebDriver, pass the details of the hub and in desired capabilities variable, we pass information for the browser, on which we want to execute our test, in this case the Firefox browser. We will discuss more about desired capabilities a little later in the chapter. So when we execute the script, the commands are sent to the hub. It fetches the information to find the node on which the actual test is to be executed and send the commands to it. In this case it will send the commands to a node which is registered with a Firefox browser:

Figure 12.11

Executing tests in parallel

To execute the tests in parallel, on the Chrome and Firefox browser together, we will initiate them. So the test execution commands will reach the hub, and the hub will direct them to their respective nodes. In this case, the tests are directed to Chrome browser machine, and Firefox browser machine:

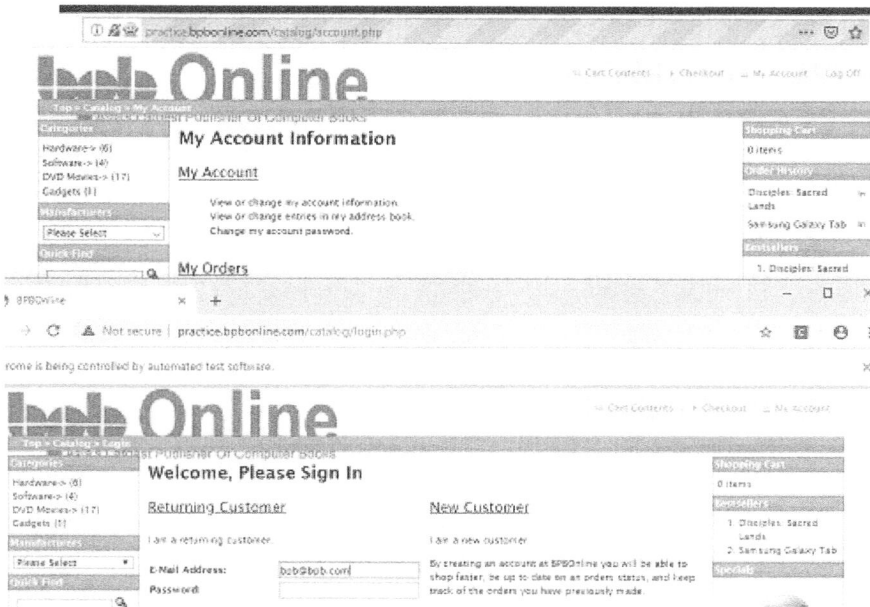

Figure 12.12

Desired capabilities

To set the test environment settings at the browser level, we have some properties associated with each browsers which we can set. So at the time of execution, whenever the browser instance will be invoked it will be set with those browser properties. Internet Explorer, Chrome, and Firefox come with their own key-value pair.

In our above test scripts, we have used desired capabilities, to set the browser key-value to Firefox or Chrome, respectively:

```
desired_capabilities={

"browserName": "firefox",}


desired_capabilities={

"browserName": "chrome",}
```

Conclusion

In this chapter we understood the usage of an important component of Selenium which allows us to run tests in parallel. We understood how we establish the Selenium server in hub mode and node mode, and instantiate the remote WebDriver at the script level to run our tests in the Grid.

Questions

1. What is a hub?
2. Explain what is a node?
3. Explain what is remote WebDriver?

Printed in Great Britain
by Amazon

43721311R00061